Appreciating Musicals

Student Book

William G. Reid

J. Weston Walch, Publisher
Portland, Maine

1   2   3   4   5   6   7   8   9   10

ISBN 0-8251-2399-2

Copyright © 1993
J. Weston Walch, Publisher
P. O. Box 658 • Portland, Maine 04104-0658

Printed in the United States of America

Contents

Introduction

In the twentieth century the United States has made major contributions to world culture: pop art in painting and sculpture, jazz and rock in music, and the musical in the theater. This book is about the story of the musical as it developed in the United States.

The first part of the book describes the various phases of musical making; writing the story, creating the lyrics, composing the music, and staging the show. The second part discusses selected musicals, decade by decade, and includes summaries of their story plots. The third part, a single chapter, looks at what happens to a musical once it has been staged.

I used several criteria to select representative musicals. Those that advanced the development of musicals, such as *Show Boat* and *Oklahoma!*, had to be included. Musicals such as *The Fantasticks* and *Pippin*, which are often used for school productions, needed to be fitted into their historical context. The opportunity to see musicals in summer stock or as revivals made certain selections necessary. Stage productions made into movies, and therefore available on television or as videos, have also influenced choices.

Yet, do not forget that this remains a selection. Year after year dozens of musicals have opened in American and British theaters. Many of those works deserve attention, but a book has only so many pages, and therefore must bypass some exciting productions. The musicals summarized in this book should encourage you to seek out others that are just as entertaining.

Most histories of the American musical begin in the nineteenth century with *The Black Crook*, because it presented a stage story with music, song, and dance. Put together from a sorry American play and a stranded French ballet company, *The Black Crook*, although popular, was more a contrivance than a solidly created musical. The opening curtain for our historical survey is on a Gilbert and Sullivan operetta. Although they were English, Gilbert and Sullivan's works enjoyed great popularity in the United States and Canada and have the ingredients from which the American musical developed.

Over the decades the United States and Great Britain traded performances and performers back and forth. English actresses Gertrude Lawrence and Julie Andrews were stars on Broadway as well as in London. English writer P. G. Wodehouse moved to the United States and achieved his first successes writing for Broadway musicals. Noel Coward's *Bitter Sweet* in the 1930's and Lionel Bart's *Oliver!* in the 1960's enjoyed success on Broadway after moving from the West End (London's theatrical district). However, this book is about the American musical theater. And, until the 1990's, when English productions began to dominate Broadway's stages, more shows sailed east from New York to London than came in the other direction.

Because the American musical defined itself following World War I, our historical survey begins in earnest from the decade of the 1920's. Three of the works from that decade's choices have been revived and songs from a fourth, *Lady, Be Good!*, are Gershwin standards.

The illustrations scattered throughout the book are based on publicity stills, posters, and other picture material from the musicals. The songs listed in the margins are major songs from the musicals mentioned in the text, and the margin comments in Part II come from reviews of the shows.

Today American musicals are performed on every continent. Film versions are seen on movie and television screens in many countries. Composers and writers abroad create works in the spirit of American musicals. Joining opera and operetta, the musical has become a form of theater to delight audiences everywhere. The stories in this book will introduce you to what some of those delights might be.

Part I

Musical Making

A musical contains many things: songs, music, story, poetry, and dance. It also contains many people: actors, actresses, singers, dancers, musicians, and artists. What appears before you as a crowded, colorful, and exciting spectacle began as a single idea months and even years earlier. How a lone idea erupts into a complex musical entertainment is the subject of the first half of this book. As you examine the process, think about how you could create a musical yourself.

Let Me Entertain You

CHAPTER 1

Musical Theater

Imagine a warm summer evening a century ago in New York City. Imagine also that you are sitting in a theater, the Fifth Avenue Theater to be exact, watching the American premiere of *The Mikado* (mĭ-ˈkahd-ō) by W. S. Gilbert and Arthur Sullivan. As the show nears its climax, a grand procession enters with the Mikado, the emperor of Japan. Awaiting him are Pooh-Bah, a high official, and Ko-Ko, the Lord High Executioner.

Be - hold the Lord High Ex - e - cu - tion-er! A
per - son - age of no - ble rank and ti - tle

The two present the Mikado with a false certificate of execution. To his horror the emperor sees that their supposed victim is his son, Nanki-Poo.

"I forget the punishment for [executing] the Heir Apparent," thunders the Mikado. "I think boiling oil occurs in it, but I'm not sure. I know it's something humorous, but lingering, with either boiling oil or melted lead...."

"Oh," moan Ko-Ko and Pooh-Bah.

"Now, let's see about your execution—will after lunch suit you? Can you wait till then?"

"Oh, yes—we can wait till then!"

"Then we'll make it after luncheon," says the Mikado.
Pooh-Bah replies, "I don't want any lunch."

Will Ko-Ko and Pooh-Bah be boiled in oil or cast in melted lead? And how did they get into this embarrassing situation in the first place? You will learn in the next chapter.

To be boiled in oil or cast in lead belongs to the world of adventure fantasy, like today's Indiana Jones movies. These punishments are not everyday events. The story of The Mikado is certainly an imaginative adventure. Musical productions like this are born in the creative imagination of the author of the story. The talent and imagination of the composer creates the music. More creative imagination brings together the stage production. Then the appreciative audience joins in the imaginative musical adventure to enjoy the show.

MUSICAL THEATER CLASSIFICATIONS

Musicals are stories acted out and sung in a theater. We see so many movies and plays that tell their stories only with acting and action, that those with songs and music seem to be the exception. Historically, however, they are the rule. Even Shakespeare wrote songs for his plays. What are the kinds of musical theater you might enjoy today? Let us see, and let's also consider how musicals differ from their musical relatives.

Opera:

Today you can attend operas in the great opera houses of Europe and America, including the Metropolitan Opera in New York City. In operas, most or all of the story is sung, regardless of whether the performer is loving, fighting, dying, laughing, or crying. Some of the musicals in this book could be considered operas. *Porgy and Bess* has been called a folk opera, and *Jesus Christ Superstar*, a rock opera. *The Phantom of the Opera* is very much an opera. Yet, growing out of the tradition of musicals, they are all a part of our story.

Operetta:

An operetta is a less serious form of opera, both in content and complexity of music. Its dialogue is spoken, not sung. When a song comes along, the performers stop talking and start singing. The operetta's subject is usually a romantic comedy. Because operettas were popular in nineteenth-century Vienna, much of their music is based on a Viennese waltz.

The Mikado, which opened this chapter, is an English operetta. Part II of this book shows how the American musical developed out of these English productions. Some modern musicals such as *The Fantasticks* and *A Little Night Music* have been called operettas.

Musical comedy: This is the term most often applied to the musicals we will examine. Musical comedies are light in theme and spiced with comedy, but their most important feature is the songs woven into the story.

So far this sounds much like operetta. But musical comedies can include many styles of music, such as jazz, pop, country, and ethnic. Songs and dances fit the story plots of musical comedies. And no matter how serious their stories, musicals are entertaining. That principle became a song by Stephen Sondheim and Jule Styne that was sung by Baby June in *Gypsy.* Its title was "Let Me Entertain You." All musical comedies need to do at least that much—entertain you with music.

Musical play: Following World War II, many composers and writers wanted to produce musicals that packed more meaning in their stories, probed deeper into the personalities of their characters, and presented more innovative music. *Fiddler on the Roof* and *Cabaret* were two such musicals. Both had their fair share of comedy, but their basic themes were not comic or romantic. In *Fiddler on the Roof* soldiers of the Russian czar (emperor) force Jews from their centuries-old home. *Cabaret* portrays Berlin during the rise of Hitler's Nazis.

Such themes could not be termed comedies, so they have been called musical plays. That does not mean they lose their entertainment value. The best of their songs are singable and memorable. But they adopt themes that are more serious than romantic or comic, and their music is more complex.

Movie musical: Hollywood has seen fit to film the most successful stage musicals. Therefore, you may be more likely to see some of the musicals described in this book as movies rather than as stage productions.

Hollywood also produced many original musicals, the majority of them only for entertainment, with stories of little depth. Some of America's best-known songs came out of Hollywood musicals, even though the films themselves have been long forgotten. We will read about a few of the best.

Should we make distinctions between musical comedies and musical plays or even operettas? Probably not. Our interest is in what makes a good musical production and what some of the best musicals are. We will introduce you to some of the musical productions that you might see in a community theater, in the movies, or on television. Therefore, let us simply call our subject **musicals.** They are mainly American, but some are British. They all have plots, laughs, romance, tears, stories, songs, dances, and above all, good music.

Questions and Activities

Examining musicals

1. Think about what musical productions you have seen, heard as a recording, or read about. Decide which are operas, operettas, and musicals.

2. If you have seen a musical on the stage, in a movie, or on TV, pick one that particularly impressed you. What stood out the most for you: the story, one of the songs, the music in general, the dances, the performers, or the scenery? Which element made the least impression?

Listening to music

1. Listen to a recording of a song from a musical, another from an opera, and a third from an operetta. How do they differ in spirit and sound?

2. Listen to a song from a Gilbert and Sullivan operetta. Which appeals most to you, words or music?

Creating a musical

At the end of each of the following chapters you will be guided in the musical-making process. You and your classmates can try some of the ideas. Your class might even decide to write and stage an original musical by following the book's suggestions.

CHAPTER 2

The Book

Katisha: You hold that I am not beautiful. But I have a left shoulder-blade that is a miracle of loveliness. People come miles to see it. My right elbow has a fascination that few can resist.

Pooh-Bah: Allow me!

Katisha: It is on view Tuesdays and Fridays, on presentation of a visiting card.

A minstrel named Nanki-Poo shows up in Titipu seeking the love of Yum-Yum. Unfortunately, Yum-Yum is engaged to Ko-Ko, her guardian. But because Ko-Ko has violated the Mikado's (emperor's) recent law against flirting, he has been condemned to death. To avoid the sentence, he appoints himself Lord High Executioner, which prevents him from cutting off his own head. That would be suicide, a capital crime. His friend Pooh-Bah has been given all other ministerial posts in Titipu.

Preparing for his wedding with Yum-Yum, Ko-Ko receives a complaint from the Mikado that there have been no executions in Titipu for a year. The desperate executioner writes a false claim that Nanki-Poo (who is really the emperor's son in disguise) has been beheaded, and he persuades the minstrel to leave Titipu. Nanki-Poo will agree only if he can marry Yum-Yum and take her with him.

The Mikado arrives in Titipu to discover that the name on the false execution certificate is that of his son. Nanki-Poo and Yum-Yum agree to return and save Ko-Ko if he marries Katisha (an elderly lady who is in love with Nanki-Poo). Preferring her to being boiled in oil or melted in lead, Ko-Ko consents. The grateful Mikado, overjoyed at seeing his son alive, forgives everyone, bringing the curtain down on *The Mikado*.

This story of Nanki-Poo's love for Yum-Yum and of Ko-Ko's dilemma comprises the **book** for Gilbert and Sullivan's *The Mikado*. The book of any musical is the story upon which it is based, the roots from which the musical tree grows. Like a tree, a musical is a single thing consisting of many parts. In place of branches, leaves, and blossoms, a musical has songs, music, dance, and scenery. A tree springs from and is nourished by its

7

unseen roots. A musical springs from and is nourished by its unread book.

The book lays down the **plot** of the musical, the route its story takes from the opening through to the conclusion. In short, it tells the story.

The actual book is more detailed than the brief story description which led off this chapter. Still, the writer of a musical's book does not construct a very complicated plot. There is just no time for it. There is too much that must go on—singing, dancing, joking—to allow for many twists and turns in the story.

Although there are exceptions, the standard musical plot involves the romantic problems of the hero and the heroine. There may be a subplot involving the more humorous romance of two secondary characters. Curly and Laurey have a serious romance in *Oklahoma!*, which ends in the death of Curly's rival. In the secondary plot, Will Parker tries to win the heart of Ado Annie, who just cannot say "No!" to any man. Sky Masterson pursues Sister Sarah in *Guys and Dolls* while Nathan Detroit and Adelaide have their difficulties because of her chronic cold.

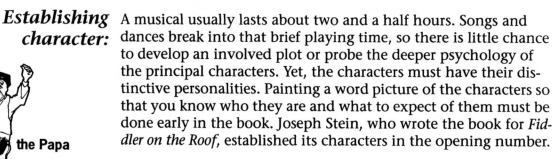

"I Cain't Say No," sings Ado Annie to Will Parker, then later tells him, give me "All Er Nothin'."

In one of their spats Adelaide tells Nathan to "Take Back Your Mink" and he tells her to go ahead, "Sue Me."

Establishing character:

the Papa

the Mama

the sons

the daughters

Yenta the matchmaker

A musical usually lasts about two and a half hours. Songs and dances break into that brief playing time, so there is little chance to develop an involved plot or probe the deeper psychology of the principal characters. Yet, the characters must have their distinctive personalities. Painting a word picture of the characters so that you know who they are and what to expect of them must be done early in the book. Joseph Stein, who wrote the book for *Fiddler on the Roof*, established its characters in the opening number.

The scene is Anatevka, a Russian village. As the villagers sing the song "Tradition," the milkman Tevye introduces himself, then his wife and their sons and daughters, describing traditional family roles. He also introduces Yenta the matchmaker, the woman who arranges marriages in Anatevka; the rabbi; a beggar; and finally, two villagers arguing over a horse trade.

You also learn from this opening song that life in Anatevka is difficult, but the people survive because of their traditions. The rabbi's prayer reveals that the people are afraid of the police serving the Russian czar (emperor).

In that seven-minute song which opens *Fiddler on the Roof*, you meet the principal characters and understand the theme. The author of the book, Joseph Stein, has quickly plunged you deeply into the plot. By the way, the music, rhythm, and dance of that opening number is exciting, colorful, and memorable.

8

Not all musicals get into the thick of the story and the introduction of characters as quickly as *Fiddler on the Roof*. But the author of a book knows there can be little delay.

Dialogue: The author of a novel or short story can describe historical background, weather, and events that affect the story. In the theater, this can be done through dance or pantomime. Scenic effects can indicate weather and time of day. However, most of what you learn about the story of a musical comes from the conversation between the performers, their **dialogue**. The plot of a musical is driven mostly by the author's dialogue.

Dialogue has additional functions. At crucial points in the story the dialogue must be ready to be turned into the lyrics of a song. Therefore, while writing the dialogue, the writer is thinking of song lyrics, and is ready to go from spoken words to sung words.

Another function of the dialogue is to ease the transition from speech to song. In everyday life you never burst into song in the middle of a friendly conversation. Yet, it happens frequently in a musical. The book must make that transition seem as natural and comfortable as possible.

The dialogue also helps establish the personality of each of the characters. A variety of speaking styles generates interest and sparkle. That in turn inspires variety in song styles arising from the dialogue.

Last, but certainly not least, dialogue provides the comedy. Regardless of how serious the theme, a musical needs comedy—be it satire, wit, understatement, overstatement, puns, put-downs, put-ons, or outright jokes. It can be in the spoken dialogue or in dialogue turned into song lyrics. The book dialogue causes the smile that can become a laugh, as these song titles suggest.

satire: "Diamonds Are a Girl's Best Friend" (*Gentlemen Prefer Blondes*)

overstatement: "The Oldest Established Permanent Floating Crap Game in New York" (*Guys and Dolls*)

understatement: "When the Idle Poor Become the Idle Rich" (*Finian's Rainbow*)

word play: "Marian the Librarian" (*The Music Man*) "Katie Went to Haiti" (*Dubarry Was a Lady*)

Sources for the book: If the book is the seed from which the musical grows, where are such seeds gathered? Some come from the fertile minds of the authors themselves. W. S. Gilbert's book for *The Mikado*, which introduced this chapter, was his original story. Original too were the stories for *Finian's Rainbow* and *The Music Man*, as well as many other musical shows.

Many more authors base a work on some outside source. As you would expect, a number of musicals have been based on straight theatrical plays. In 1943, Oscar Hammerstein II took Lynn Riggs's play *Green Grow the Lilacs* and turned it into the book for *Oklahoma!*, a production that changed the direction of American musicals with its combination of music, song, dance, and a detailed plot. Just as distinctive was the book of *My Fair Lady*, which closely followed its source, George Bernard Shaw's play *Pygmalion*.

A playwright who has contributed many works for modern musicals is, as unlikely as it may seem, William Shakespeare. *The Boys From Syracuse* is not about a football or basketball team from that upstate New York university. Instead, the 1938 musical concerned Syracuse, Sicily, in the time of ancient Greece, and was based on Shakespeare's *Comedy of Errors*. Cole Porter turned Shakespeare's *The Taming of the Shrew* into *Kiss Me Kate* in 1948. The ultimate Shakespeare musical was *West Side Story*, in which Arthur Laurents's book brought *Romeo and Juliet* to the streets of New York's West Side.

If it seems that choosing Shakespeare as a book partner means making a successful musical, it is not necessarily the case. One of the least-remembered Rodgers and Hammerstein musicals is their 1953 show *Me and Juliet*, also adapted from Shakespeare's romantic tragedy.

Like plays, novels would seem to be a likely source for a musical book. A year after Edna Ferber's novel *Show Boat* was a 1926 best seller, Oscar Hammerstein II adapted it for the historical musical you will read about in Chapter 9. In the early 1960's, Lionel Bart borrowed from Charles Dickens's century-old novel *Oliver Twist* to write the book for the musical *Oliver!*. The 1966 Broadway musical hit *Mame* was based on Patrick Dennis's book *Auntie Mame*, published in 1954.

The short story is another form of fiction upon which one could base the book for a musical. Russian-born Shalom Aleichem wrote many short stories about Eastern European village life. Joseph Stein used one of them as a source for *Fiddler on the Roof*. A world away from Aleichem's peasant villages was Broadway of the

1930's and its bookies, gamblers, hustlers, and show girls. Damon Runyon wrote short stories about them, which Abe Burrows used for *Guys and Dolls*.

Many Broadway musicals have been made into movies. A few movies have reversed the procedure and served as the book for musicals. In the 1930's the fabled Greta Garbo starred in a movie entitled *Ninotchka*, which Cole Porter used for his last stage musical, *Silk Stockings*, in 1955. Hugh Wheeler turned Ingmar Bergman's 1955 film *Smiles of a Summer Night* into the 1973 musical *A Little Night Music*.

The comic strips seem a surprising source for the book of a musical. Yet there is Charlie Brown of the *Peanuts* strip despairing in *You're a Good Man, Charlie Brown*, Little Orphan Annie dancing in *Annie*, and hillbilly Li'l Abner clod-hopping in the 1957 musical *Li'l Abner*. As long ago as 1908, Victor Herbert composed the music for *Little Nemo*, based on that pioneering comic strip in the *New York Herald*.

Musical book ideas can come from almost anywhere, it seems. In the 1930's, novelist John O'Hara wrote a series of fictitious letters for *The New Yorker* magazine. They were supposedly written by a Chicago nightclub operator. Each letter closed with the signature, "From your pal, Joey." In 1940 O'Hara collaborated with Richard Rodgers and Lorenz Hart to base the musical *Pal Joey* on those letters.

> Joey not only writes letters but tells how "I Could Write a Book" with lines to flatter women.

The lesson of this brief survey is that when the writers of book musicals have turned to outside sources, they have made strong choices. All have vivid main characters—Oliver Twist, Juliet, Pal Joey, and Charlie Brown, to name a few. Their stories are familiar; therefore, it does not take long to introduce the characters and establish atmosphere. The plots are already in place. A style of dialogue has been established that can influence that of the musical.

A strong idea or a solid source for the book sets the creation of the musical in motion. Upon the book the musical builds, the plot turns, the songs sing, the dances prance. The book comes first. From that book come the lyrics.

Questions and Activities

Examining musicals

1. Select a story you know—a novel, short story, play, movie, or other source. Make a brief outline of the plot, then underline the following items:

    a. The place where the theme or story problem first becomes clear

    b. Where principal characters are introduced

    c. Where the story problem is resolved

2. Try to see the logic of the placement of these points in the plot.

Listening to music

1. Listen to the recorded songs of a musical. Decide the following:

    a. Which song states the show's theme?

    b. Which songs help establish the personality of any character?

Creating a musical

Think of a source for adaptation as a musical. It could be a novel, short story, TV program, comic strip, or something else that appeals to you. Decide how strong your source is in the following features:

    a. Do the characters in your source have vivid, distinct personalities?

    b. Has your source a clear theme, purpose, or message? What is it?

    c. Does your source include conversation that can become the dialogue and lyrics of a musical?

    d. Does the source have variety in the following?
        1. plot
        2. character types
        3. dialogue styles

    e. What sort of comedy does your source offer—light, heavy, dark, satirical, slapstick?

CHAPTER 3

Lyrics

On a tree by a river a little tom-tit
Sang "Willow, titwillow, titwillow!"

The previous chapter opened with an excerpt from "the book" for Gilbert and Sullivan's *The Mikado*. Toward the end of the story Ko-Ko must convince Katisha to marry him, or else lose his life. To break down her reluctance, Ko-Ko sings her a song about a despairing bird, a melancholy tom-tit.

And I said to him "Dicky-bird, why do you sit
Singing "Willow, titwillow, titwillow?"
"Is it weakness of intellect, birdie?" I cried,
"Or a rather tough worm in your little inside?"
With a shake of his poor little head, he replied,
"Oh, willow, titwillow, titwillow!"

Having written the book for *The Mikado*, Gilbert turned to developing the lyrics for the songs. Ko-Ko's plea for marriage gave him the place to develop a tongue-in-cheek love song. His poetic device was a lovesick bird with suicidal tendencies.

With book in hand, the musical begins to grow. The most important task is creating its songs, for that is what a musical is all about. A song is made from melody and lyrics.

Have you ever wondered which is written first, the music or the words of the song? That question sounds like asking which comes first, the chicken or the egg. The answer is, sometimes the lyrics come first, sometimes the music comes first, and sometimes they are created together. It is interesting to look at songs for which either the music or lyrics were created first, because that helps us understand the music-making process. For this reason, we'll return to the issue again in this and the next chapter.

Functions of lyrics:

Express emotions

Many songs develop from the dialogue already outlined or written in the book. This is especially true of solos and duets, particularly at emotional moments in the dialogue, such as when a character discovers he or she has fallen in love. Tony sings joyously of having met "Maria" in *West Side Story*. At the end of *My Fair Lady*, Professor Higgins, surprised at himself, sings "I've Grown Accustomed to Her Face," when he realizes he has become fond of Eliza. Song lyrics often take over from spoken dialogue to express emotions.

Establish character

Lyrics also help establish the character of a role. At the very beginning of *My Fair Lady*, two songs help paint the character portraits of the two principals, Professor Higgins and Eliza Doolittle. The professor, a scholar of linguistics, asks, "Why Can't the English?" learn to speak their language correctly. This positions him as a learned person, cultured, but also something of a class snob. Immediately thereafter, Eliza sings "Wouldn't It Be Loverly?" in a Cockney dialect, setting her up as the very type of person the professor despises. The two contrasting lyrics establish character and at the same time set up the personality conflict that the book sets out to resolve.

When the crippled beggar Porgy sings "I Got Plenty o' Nuttin'" in *Porgy and Bess*, you realize that he is poor but accepts his lot in life.

In *Hello, Dolly!*, the boisterous lady first sings "I Put My Hand In" just about everything and everybody's business, letting you know she is an irritating meddler. Because song lyrics are more expressive than spoken speech, you understand the character of a role very quickly when it is sung.

Establish setting

The early pages of a novel or short story establish the mood of the story and its setting. In a musical production, a song lyric usually does the job. *Porgy and Bess* opens with a young mother singing about "Summertime," the season of easy living when catfish jump and cotton grows.

It is summer too in *Oklahoma!* The opening lyric celebrates it with "Oh What a Beautiful Morning!," bringing an upbeat tone to the musical setting. The corn as high as an elephant's eye depicts a rural landscape of bounty and optimism.

Establish theme

Lyrics help establish the theme early in a musical. *Hair* opens with "Aquarius," in which we learn that a new age is dawning. Something new is about to happen in the musical and in the age of harmony, trust, sympathy, and understanding that it is proclaiming.

When you meet Don Quixote in *Man of La Mancha*, he tells you about his goals as the "Man of La Mancha." This establishes his character while contributing to the theme of the show. In the second act we realize his quest may be in vain, for he states it as "The Impossible Dream." As he lies dying, the two songs reinforce the themes.

Pacing and entertainment

Songs help pace the musical. The audience has come to the theater to hear songs, so they should not be left too long without hearing one.

Pacing also means changing the tempo of the story. If the theme has been heavy and the songs emotional, an entertaining song can change the pace and lighten the spirit before returning to the serious business of the story. Comical songs use funny lyrics set to a snappy beat.

Will Parker returns to *Oklahoma!* from Kansas City at the moment Curly and Laurey are having romance problems. Will describes how everything is up-to-date in "Kansas City." There, they even have indoor bathrooms, which means you can go to the privy without getting your feet wet.

In *Fiddler on the Roof*, Tevye watches his beloved traditions crumble as his daughters marry against his wishes and the police disrupt one of the weddings. The poor milkman asks his weary wife, "Do You Love Me?" Exasperated, she describes how she has worked every day, all day, to cook, clean, and raise their children, and he asks such a silly question.

With a toe-tapping rhythm backed up by a honky-tonk piano, King Herod reels off clever, witty lines in his song in *Jesus Christ Superstar*. It falls between the song sung when Jesus first appears before Pilate and the song about the death of Judas. The change of pace is obvious, from a slow, cynical number to Herod's swinging showstopper to a song of death.

Pace in a musical is important. The show must not drag. It must drive forward. Much goes on in the several hours of a musical—the story, songs, dance, and jokes all chasing one another across the stage. In low gear or high gear, song lyrics drive the musical ahead.

The lyricist: The writer of the musical's book has helped the lyricist by anticipating pace, building emotional peaks into the plot, and describing atmosphere and settings. The lyricist turns these elements into the poetry of the songs.

The lyricist and the writer of the book are frequently the same person. Therefore, that single person thinks of lyrics even as he or she is writing the book. Oscar Hammerstein II wrote both book and lyrics for all of the great musicals he created with Richard Rodgers. Dorothy Donnelly wrote the book and lyrics for *The Student Prince* and Tom Jones did the same for *The Fantasticks*. But our interest here is with the writer as lyricist, not as creator of the book.

The chicken-or-the-egg question

SOUTH PACIFIC

Let us ask that question once again. Which is created *first*, the words or the music of a song? The manner in which Richard Rodgers and Oscar Hammerstein II worked can help us with the answer (or maybe, confuse the answer).

Long before collaborating on *Oklahoma!* in 1943, the two men had worked with others. Rodgers had composed music for the lyrics written by Lorenz Hart for such shows as *On Your Toes* and *The Boys From Syracuse*. During the same period, Hammerstein had written lyrics for songs by George Gershwin, Sigmund Romberg, Rudolf Friml, and Jerome Kern.

In his collaboration with Hart, Rodgers composed the music for a song, then Hart wrote the words. The same was true in Hammerstein's case, for his composer partners first created the music for their shows. Given the melodies, Hammerstein then wrote the lyrics. So our question might be answered, the music comes first, then the words of the songs.

But not always! Once Rodgers and Hammerstein began working together on musicals such as *Oklahoma!*, *Carousel*, and *South Pacific*, they reversed their procedures. Hammerstein first wrote the book. Next, he decided where the songs should occur, then he

16

wrote the words. When he had finished the lyrics, he handed them to Rodgers, who then wrote the music.

Lyric technique

The words of a song are poems, but the lyricist is not as free as other poets. The lyrics must be fitted into the musical clothing that the composer tailors. The stitches in the poem are made with rhythm. The rhythm of the poem depends on word accents.

In any word of two or more syllables, one syllable is accented. In a song, that accent falls in a standard pattern. Here are more lines from the song that opened this chapter. The spoken accents have been marked in the first two lines. You see the pattern of two unaccented syllables followed by an accented one. Read the lines that follow to see how this pattern continues. The pattern of accents becomes the rhythm.

> He slapped at his chest, as he sat on that bough,
> Singing, "Wil-low, tit-wil-low, tit-wil-low."
> And a cold perspiration bespangled his brow,
> "Oh, willow, titwillow, titwillow!"

The lyricist does not labor over these accents. Instead, he or she has a sense of rhythm and creates the lyric by letting this practiced sense guide the writing. Upon this rhythm in the lyrics the composer can anchor the song's melody.

There is a second kind of pattern woven into the lyrics, that of rhyming words. Lyricists use rhyming words to focus on a special part of the song's message, set up a joke, bring a song to a satisfactory conclusion, or simply have fun.

> He sobbed and he sighed, and a gurgle he gave,
> Then he threw himself into the billowy wave,
> And an echo arose from the suicide's grave—
> "Oh, willow, titwillow, titwillow!"

gave
wave
grave

You have no difficulty identifying the rhyming pattern of "gave," "wave," and "grave" ending the lines of Gilbert's song for Ko-Ko. The rhyme pattern and rhythm pattern stitch the lyric into a spoken sequence that can become a song.

Because of these two patterns, many composers prefer that the lyrics be created first. The lyrics then give them rhythm patterns to work with, because music also consists of sounds arranged in a patterned sequence. Therefore, a logical order in the creation of the musical would be to develop lyrics from the book, then compose the music for those lyrics.

17

However, we have seen that this order of lyrics first, music second, is not always followed. Some composer-writer teams prefer to do it the other way around. So we are not finished with the problem of which comes first. Now it is time to meet the other half of the team: the composer, the person who makes the music. After all, music is the most important ingredient of any musical.

Questions and Activities

Examining musicals

1. Note again the accented syllables of the song "Titwillow" on page 17. Test the song's consistency by seeing if the same pattern fits the second set of words on that page.

2. Describe the rhyming pattern in the song "Titwillow."

3. A lyricist paces the song sequence in a musical by varying tempo and style from fast to slow, serious to entertaining, theme song to comedy song to love song. Look at the names of the songs on the liner notes of a recording of a musical. Do the titles suggest this pace change?

4. Look at the bands separating songs on a record album of a musical show, or note the playing times for the songs. Do shorter songs alternate with longer ones? If so, this is another example of song pacing.

Listening to music

1. Listen to five of your favorite songs, not necessarily from a musical. State the theme of each.

2. Pick one of those five songs and write down the words. Can you find the rhythmic and rhyming patterns in the lyrics?

Creating a musical

1. Pick an important section in the book outline you made for the previous chapter. Expand that section by creating a speech for one of the characters. Then try to turn that speech into a poem that could become a song lyric.

2. If your class wants to create a musical, choose one of the books written for the previous chapter. Each class member can then pick out an important section of the book to expand into a poem, as in the activity above.

CHAPTER 4

Songs

KO-KO

1. On a tree by a riv-er a lit-tle tom-tit Sang——

"Wil-low, tit-wil-low, tit - wil - low" And I said to him, "Dick - y - bird,

why do you sit Sing - ing 'Wil-low, tit - wil - low, tit -

wil- low'?" "Is it weak - ness of in - tel - lect, bird - ie?" I cried, "Or a

rath - er tough worm in your lit - tle in - side?" With a

shake of his poor lit - tle head, he re - plied, "Oh,

wil - low, tit-wil - low, tit - wil - low!"

Sir William Gilbert wrote the poem for the satirical love ballad "Titwillow," then Sir Arthur Sullivan set the words to music. As in all of their productions, Gilbert first wrote the lyrics for which Sullivan composed the music.

Richard Rodgers and Oscar Hammerstein II also followed this procedure for such great musicals as *Oklahoma!*, *Carousel*, and *South Pacific*. At lunch one day while working on *South Pacific*, Hammerstein handed Rodgers a typewritten sheet with the lyrics for a song to be called "Bali Ha'i." Rodgers turned the sheet over, and in five minutes wrote the melody for the song on the back. The lyrics came first, then just that quickly came the music.

However, we have seen that the creative process can work in the opposite way. Let us look at some more examples. When Oscar Hammerstein II worked with his first partner, Jerome Kern, to write such songs as "Make Believe" and "Ol' Man River" for *Show Boat* and "The Song Is You" for *Music in the Air*, he wrote the lyrics to the melodies Kern had already written. Here are two more examples to demonstrate how creators of musicals work.

One involved Victor Herbert and his lyricist Henry Blossom. During a concert appearance in Saratoga, New York (once a fashionable summer resort), Herbert was visited by Blossom. The two were preparing *Mlle. Modiste*. Agreeing that the operetta needed a genuine showstopper, they struggled but failed to come up with an idea. As Herbert was about to fall asleep a few nights later, an idea crossed his mind. He got out of bed, wrote down the melody he had thought of, then fell asleep. The following day he gave Blossom the song, and Blossom then wrote the lyrics that became "Kiss Me Again," the hit of the show and one of the best-known of their songs. This time the melody inspired the words.

What about the person such as Meredith Willson or Cole Porter who is both composer and lyricist? Porter's method was to create music and lyrics together, working at the piano and jotting down words as a song developed. He generally worked first on the opening of the song and then its closing. Those done, he worked from the beginning and the ending toward the middle to complete the song.

We must conclude that there is no set rule about how to write a musical, except that whatever works best for the musical's collaborators is the proper procedure.

Composing techniques: Kern and Hammerstein's 1932 show *Music in the Air* tells of a mountain boy and his girlfriend who walked to Munich to sell his song. In "The Song Is You" another composer tries to impress on the girl that she has become his musical inspiration. A person *could* inspire a song. But more likely inspiration lies with the show's book or the song's lyrics.

To a person who is not a composer, creating music seems like a magical act, and Rodgers, who reportedly composed "Bali Ha'i" in five minutes, must have been a wizard. But such people develop their magic through years of experience with music, and their minds are ready to snatch at musical ideas whenever the need arises. Hammerstein's poem "Bali Ha'i" suggested the mystery of an island paradise. Rodgers drew from his long experience of working with music to paint a melodic picture of that exotic image.

Musical images

O O O O - k
     la
      hom a

A song lyric can give a composer a musical clue. That is why many want words first to suggest the melodic sounds the song might take.

Through experience, a composer knows what kinds of melodies will achieve these descriptive sounds. A lyric poem that expresses triumph, glory, freedom, or some similar joyful, uplifting feeling is best carried by a wide-ranging melody. Just such a song is Rodgers' melody for the song "Oklahoma!," which concludes that musical. Its melody ranges high and low, skipping notes as it dives down then leaps up the musical scale. Listen to it or to Jerry Herman's song "Hello, Dolly!" from the musical of that name to hear how such spirited melodies work.

If Ev-er I Would Leave You

On the other hand, a melody that moves slowly up and down the scale without making great leaps in pitch promotes a smooth, gliding feeling. The melody sounds more intimate, more inward, more romantic. Such is Frederick Loewe's melody for Alan Jay Lerner's lyrics of "If Ever I Would Leave You" from *Camelot*. No great pitch jumps here.

On the following page is the song melody that Victor Herbert thought up that night in Saratoga. Notice how succeeding notes lie near one another on the scale as long as the lyrics express the soft summer night and soulful feelings. But once the couple embrace, then kiss, there is a leap in tone ("tenderly pressed") then a drop ("close to your"), a leap again ("kiss"), another down ("me"), then up and down. The melody expresses the joy of the kiss.

21

Kiss Me Again

words by Henry Blossom
music by Victor Herbert

Sweet sum-mer breeze, whis-per-ing trees, Stars shin-ing soft-ly a-bove____; Ros-es in bloom, waft-ed per-fume, Sleep-y birds dream-ing of love____. Safe in your arms, far from a-larms, Day-light shall come but in vain____. Ten-der-ly pressed close to your breast, Kiss me! Kiss me a-gain, Kiss me a-gain, Kiss me, kiss me a-gain____.

Sweet summer breeze, whispering trees,
Stars shining softly above;
Roses in bloom, wafted perfume,
Sleepy birds dreaming of love

Speech melody

Spoken speech also inspires melody. Language has its natural melody of rising and falling tones as one speaks. A composer often exaggerates language's natural melody to create a song.

Say "On a tree by a river," the first phrase of "Titwillow," the chapter's opening song. Does your voice rise on the word "tree," then fall again to "river"? Sullivan used that natural rise and fall to begin the song's melody.

Read aloud Gilbert's poem for "Titwillow" while noting the rise and fall of the melody on the musical scale. Does it follow the natural, spoken melody? It might or might not. But spoken melody can help the musical melody along.

22

Musical rhythm

Rhythm complements melody. With lyrics in hand, the composer already has a rhythm with which to work. In the previous chapter you read about how repeated accents create the lyric's rhythm. The composer transposes this rhythm to the song.

Look again at the song "Titwillow," which opened this chapter. The musical symbols tell a performer how to sing or play Sullivan's song. In Chapter 3 you marked the word accents of the lyrics of the song. If you compare those with the musical symbols, you may notice that those word accents fall on the first and fourth count of each measure. The lyric rhythm now becomes the song's rhythm. If you are not familiar with musical symbols, the following chart explains them to you.

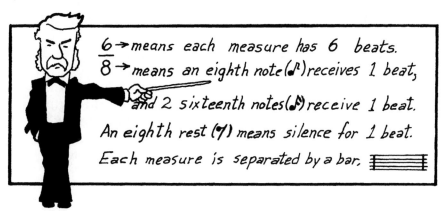

$\frac{6}{8}$ → means each measure has 6 beats.

8 → means an eighth note (♪) receives 1 beat, and 2 sixteenth notes (♬) receive 1 beat. An eighth rest (⅞) means silence for 1 beat. Each measure is separated by a bar.

If the procedure is reversed and the music is composed first, then the lyricist fits word accents of the lyric to the musical rhythm.

Functions of melody and rhythm:

Expressing atmosphere

Rhythm affects the atmosphere of the musical situation. If the song sings of a spirited moment, the rhythm is catchy. If it sings of a serious moment, the rhythm is slower, heavier.

Rhythm does much for the setting of a song. The story of *Carousel* occurs in a nineteenth-century Maine fishing village. The spirited "The Carousel Waltz" gets the musical started. The rhythm of a waltz, the nineteenth century's most popular dance, helps establish the period setting for the story.

The rhythm of a march is not only spirited but also helps set the scene for small-town America at the turn of the century. That is certainly the Iowa setting for the march rhythm of "Seventy-six Trombones" in *The Music Man*.

23

However, march and waltz rhythms are not for Berger when he sings "Donna" or for Hud when he sings "Colored Spade" in *Hair*. Instead, rock rhythms fit the time, place, and attitude.

Melody also supports the mood of a scene. "Bali Ha'i" uses half-note steps in its melody to suggest an exotic island. "Summertime" opens *Porgy and Bess* with a lullaby for warm, lazy summer days.

Expressing emotions

With how many different feelings can the phrase "kiss me" be said? It can be spoken timidly, hopefully, joyfully, and so on. However, if you sing the words "kiss me," your emotions sound even stronger. Look at Herbert's song "Kiss Me Again." Play it on an instrument or sing it and decide what sort of spirit it expresses.

This little kissing exercise demonstrates one function of a song. It expresses the intended emotion in an emphatic way. Love, sadness, joy, disappointment, revelation, depression, and triumph are expressed through song. "I Get a Kick Out Of You" (*Anything Goes*), "Bewitched, Bothered and Bewildered" (*Pal Joey*) and "June Is Bustin' Out All Over" (*Carousel*) suggest the emotions they express in their lyrics.

Expressing personality

Like lyrics, music helps express the personality of a character. Professor Harold Hill is a brassy salesman and confidence man in *The Music Man*. You understand this personality when he sings "Seventy-six Trombones," a spirited, aggressive march. Composer Meredith Willson used the same melody but sweetened the rhythm for quiet, pretty Marian to sing "Good-night My Someone." When Hill falls in love with Marian, he sings her love song, expressing his changed feelings and personality. Marian then surprises everyone with an unexpected assertiveness as she switches to "Seventy-six Trombones." The same melody with different rhythms expresses the differing personalities as the story progresses.

The song "It Ain't Necessarily So" allows Sportin' Life to strut out his sly, cocky personality in *Porgy and Bess*.

A song in a musical has more to do than just entertain. It is one reason that the music of a show might be very successful without producing any single popular chart tune. The music, like the lyrics, serves the story outlined in the book.

The music of a song performs the same function as the lyrics it carries. It can establish mood, setting, emotion, and personality. Having done that, it might just be a very good song, memorable enough to become a standard, still sung or played long after the musical is no longer performed. It might be a great song.

Questions and Activities

Examining musicals

1. Here are the lyrics for another song from *The Mikado*. If you have never heard the song, try to compose a melody for it using its spoken melody as a guide. The original Sullivan melody appears at the beginning of the next chapter.

   "The Wand'ring Minstrel"

   A wand'ring minstrel I—
   A thing of shreds and patches,
   Of ballads, songs and snatches,
   And dreamy lullaby!

2. Analyze the matching rhythm patterns of the lyrics and melody of "Kiss Me Again" as seen in this chapter.

Listening to music

1. If possible, listen to songs from *The Mikado* or another Gilbert and Sullivan work. How do the melodies fit the spirit of the lyrics?

2. This chapter has mentioned a number of songs—"Bali Ha'i," "Oklahoma," "Seventy-six Trombones," and "June Is Bustin' Out All Over" among them. Listen to these or others available on record and decide whether the music fits the spirit of the lyrics.

Creating a musical

1. Compose a melody for the lyric you wrote in the previous chapter. Sing your song into a tape recorder, work it out on a piano, or write it out as music.

2. If your class is creating a musical, each lyricist can work out a melody for his or her song. If that seems difficult, maybe lyrics can be fitted to known songs. Then work together as a class, adjusting the song melodies so that they fit your musical.

CHAPTER 5

The Score

Imagine again that the year is 1885 and you are attending the American premiere of *The Mikado*. Before the curtain rises, the orchestra plays the overture, an arrangement of the show's music for the time during which the audience settles into their seats. This particular segment is the melody of Nanki-Poo's song "The Wand'ring Minstrel."

Types of music: The overture is one of several types of musical arrangements played during the show. Together with the songs, all of the music you hear played in a musical is called the **score**. Here are the kinds of music that make up the score.

The overture

As just described, the overture is the orchestral music heard before the curtain opens. It is an arrangement of songs taken from the show. In the overture, slow numbers usually alternate with fast pieces to set the musical pace for the show. The overture allows latecomers to settle in their seats, gives a taste of what is to come, and puts the audience into the spirit of the performance.

In recent years some directors have not begun with overtures, preferring to dive into the story with the first note of music.

Opening number

The first piece after the curtain opens generally states the theme of the musical, introduces some of the characters, or establishes the setting. It might perform just one of these functions or all three.

In Chapter 2 you read about how Tevye introduces himself, his family, and fellow villagers with the song "Tradition," the opening number of *Fiddler on the Roof. Guys and Dolls* opens with a ballet portraying the bustling activity of Times Square, establishing its New York setting. Then three racetrack touts sing "A Fugue for Tinhorns," introducing its gambling theme. *West Side Story* also opens with a ballet as two rival street gangs face off, spotlighting the major plot conflict. Each of these opening numbers makes a musical statement that sets the story in motion.

Straight songs

The majority of the songs in a musical are standard: love songs, ballads, and so on. You examined the making of such songs in the previous chapter. The composer of the score promotes musical variety by alternating or mixing song styles as the show progresses. Two or three slow ballads in a row, no matter how important the message of the lyrics, can promote boredom. The many songs of *Hair* borrowed sounds from New Orleans, Memphis, Nashville, Liverpool, and even India. Song variety aids pacing and prevents yawns.

Chorus songs

Most songs are sung as a solo by one of the lead performers or as a duet by two of the stars. Ensemble songs require a trio or quartet. Frequently the whole company joins in singing as a chorus. A song that begins as a solo might shift into a chorus song.

Audiences love chorus songs. The sound is big and, if the song includes dancing, the effect is colorful. Chorus songs are usually rousing numbers, triumphal, hopeful, grand in sound and expression. Chorus songs pull everyone into the act, the whole population of wherever the story is set: Russian villagers, Maine fishermen, Oklahoma farmers, or New York street people. A chorus number makes the audience feel it is part of the stage experience. When the heroine or hero sings, the people in the theater watch and listen. When a chorus sings, they feel like joining in. They are drawn into the story.

Rhythm songs

When your feet start tapping or your fingers begin rapping the arm of your theater seat, you are listening to a rhythm song. Rhythm pushes lyrics rapidly ahead. Rhythm is fun. Rhythm is exciting. Rhythm is catching. Songs such as "Luck Be a Lady Tonight" from *Guys and Dolls* or "If I Were a Rich Man" from *Fiddler on the Roof*—even their titles have a snappy rhythm. Rhythm songs leave an audience delightedly exhausted.

Patter songs

When Rex Harrison was cast in the role of Professor Higgins in *My Fair Lady*, the star was an actor but not a singer. Harrison only accepted the role after he was shown that his numbers would be patter songs. Such songs have a narrow melodic range delivered in a sing-song manner with tightly strung, rhyming lyrics. The delight of such songs is their fast-paced patter.

With *The Music Man*, Meredith Willson wrote patter songs for veteran movie actor Robert Preston, whose rapid, pitchman delivery ignited the show.

Dance music

Music for the show's dances can range from fast, colorful production numbers with much movement to slow dances that adapt classical ballet to the musical stage. Music for the dances should entertain, but it must also inspire dance movements of beauty and visual meaning. The following chapter looks more deeply into the use of dance in musicals.

Background music

The orchestra plays background music between scenes or while some muted action takes place on the stage. Background music can create mood. It can serve as a transition from one scene to another. Repeating a melody that was played earlier recalls the song's earlier message or points out the reappearance of a particular character.

Reprise

The reprise (ri-ˈprēz) is a song from earlier in the performance sung again with the same words, or with new words fitted to the previous melody. It is frequently one of the best songs in the show, which pleases the audience. It generally restates the theme of the book or sums up the moral of the story. In the second half of *The Sound of Music*, Maria, Captain Von Trapp, and the children sing the title song, which Maria had sung alone earlier in the musical. The reprise points out the beauty of the Austrian mountains even as the family flees the ugliness of Nazism.

Although usually heard at the end, the reprise can also occur earlier, often in the second act, tying it to an idea heard before.

Finale

A reprise might lead into the finale (fi-ˈnah-lee) or be a part of it. The finale is generally upbeat in spirit. It closes the story, if not with a happy ending, at least with a feeling that the problem has been solved. The hero and heroine are there, probably with the whole population of the show, chorus and dancers, sending the audience away feeling that life has been made a little better for having spent the evening at a musical.

Composer of the score: The score includes all of the music arranged for the performance. It is based on and includes the songs created by the composer. The score can be written by the composer. Or it may be composed by the musical director of the show, the musical arranger, or another person who does the orchestrations. Still, the composer of the songs remains the prime musical creator, since he or she creates the melodies which are expanded into the score.

Here is how one composer works. He is Andrew Lloyd Webber, the young composer of *Jesus Christ Superstar*, who went on to a successful career creating the music for *Evita*, *Cats* (left), *The Phantom of the Opera*, and other successful musicals.

Webber begins with a line of melody that he plans to develop into a complete song. That, in turn, he will expand as a part of the score. He creates the single melody to fit the mood and theme of the action at its particular place in the book. Then, using piano or synthesizer and a tape recorder, Webber tries dozens, even hundreds of variations on that invented melodic line. He expands it, plays with the chords, adjusts its rhythm and pacing.

Having done this for a single song, he then works that melodic line into the development of the complete score, using it in combination with the melodies from the work's other songs. He continues adjusting, changing, developing that germ of a musical idea until he is finally assured that he has created a satisfactory musical score.

The score is the complete musical package of the show. All other parts of the musical may be successful, but if the score is weak, the musical fails.

Roots: Lloyd Webber, who was the most successful composer of musicals in the 1980's, is British, not American. Nevertheless, his scores have grown from the roots of the American musical as well as European music. Most of the song types described in this chapter come from European operas and operettas—they too contain solos, duets, chorus numbers, reprises, and finales. However, the score of a musical is unique in its variety of musical styles and vigorous rhythms.

The particular rhythms of American musicals can be traced back through jazz to blues and ragtime, music that has developed out of African-American culture. Without those roots, the score of the American musical would not be much different from European opera or operetta.

That distinctive musical score is "the sound of music" that the audience has come to the theater to hear.

Questions and Activities

Examining musicals

1. Look at the song titles listed on the record covers of musicals. Decide which song probably states the theme of each musical, then name that theme. Listen to the song to see if your guess was correct.

2. The purpose of an overture is to put an audience into the spirit of the coming performance, although in recent years some musicals have begun without an overture. Think of reasons overtures may not be desired or thought necessary.

Listening to music

1. Listen to the songs on a recording of a musical, then answer these questions.

    a. What purpose does the opening song serve?

    b. Which are chorus songs and why were they chosen not to be sung solo?

    c. Which song is sung later as a reprise? Why this particular song?

    d. Why was the last song chosen to close the show?

2. If you can hear the full score of a musical, try to identify melodies from songs in the overture, background music, or transitional music (the music between major stage events and numbers).

Creating a musical

1. From the songs or lyrics the class has prepared in the previous chapters, decide which would best be sung as solos, duets, or chorus numbers.

2. Which songs in the class musical might be reprised?

3. Would any of the class songs be better performed as a patter song than with a sung melody?

4. If melodies have been created for the class songs, which ones might be used as part of the overture? In what order would they be used in the overture?

CHAPTER 6

Dance

"Three little maids from school are we,"

Yum-Yum, Peep-Bo, and Pitti-Sing toddle on stage with small, dainty steps, followed by a chorus of women stepping pitty-pat in the same Oriental fashion.

"Three little maids from school are we,
Pert as a school-girl well can be,
Filled to the brim with girlish glee,
*   Three little maids from school!"*

Their tiny steps give character to Yum-Yum, her two sisters, and former school friends. The steps define them as demure, gentle, and feminine. Stylized movement like Yum-Yum's delicate walk, when set to the rhythm of a song—

"Life is a joke that's just begun!
*   Three little maids from school!*

—becomes a dance.

The waltz was the standard theater dance when Gilbert and Sullivan wrote *The Mikado*. However, dance interpretation can take many forms. Jazz-based dance invaded the world of Yum-Yum when the operetta was restaged in 1939 as *The Hot Mikado* with an all African-American cast.

Much of the special quality of the American musical is rooted in African-American heritage. The jazz rhythms of American show music certainly come from black music traditions. So do the athletic, rapid, leaping steps of American show dancing.

Until British musicals began dominating the 1980's, critics felt only Americans could dance the lively production numbers of musicals. That American dance talent can be traced back over a

33

century and a half to a single performer. In the years before the Civil War the popular show dance was the Irish jig. In the 1840's, William Henry Lane, known as Juba, made a living as one of the first black entertainers in the United States. Lane added African-American rhythms to the popular jig, creating a new and exciting dance form, the tap dance. In the copy of a mid-nineteenth-century engraving at the left, Lane does his dance. The tap dance has been an American exhibition dance ever since, from the variety show dances of Bill "Bojangles" Robinson to the movie routines of Fred Astaire.

Juba Lane's contribution was more than just the invention of the tap dance. Just as important was his demonstration of how dance programs could be created by combining European and African traditions into a new American dance style. Nothing profited more from this marriage than the American musical.

Tap dance, jazz dance, and the waltz are used in musicals to support the book plot and entertain. But how can you tell a story with dance? By linking movement—action—to musical rhythm.

Make a simple move. Snap your fingers.

Fingers snap and an angry street gang leaps onto the stage. With snapping fingers the opening mood of *West Side Story* is established. The dance expresses cockiness and fear, street passions that set the steel-trap tension of the musical.

Functions of dance

Like lyrics and music, dance can create an atmosphere. The music of the dance establishes the mood, which the dancers' movements amplify into a romantic duet or a rousing carnival festival or the tense conflict that opens *West Side Story*.

Like lyrics and music, dance can also replace dialogue. Again, *West Side Story*: The hero, Tony, and the heroine, Maria, meet for the first time at a dance in the high school gym. When they meet, they fall in love, their feelings expressed as they dance. Later in the story Tony and Maria sing of "Somewhere" that they can live free of street prejudice. Their song becomes a ballet expressing hope through dance rather than words.

Dance can move story plot along. When the Jets and Sharks meet for the climactic fight that ends in death, the action is performed as dance. Although this could have been a straight action sequence, the fight as a dance is more intense, emotional, and memorable.

The man who conceived the original idea for the musical was Jerome Robbins, a dancer and choreographer (kōr-ē-ˈog-rǎ-fur), or dance designer. Not only did he **choreograph** (ˈkōr-ē-ǎ-graf) the dance sequences, but he directed the entire musical. Carol Lawrence, who played Maria, had been a soloist for the Chicago Opera ballet. Seldom has dance been used as effectively in a musical production as in *West Side Story*.

Dance movements:  Let's return to the snapping fingers that open *West Side Story*. Try an experiment by snapping your fingers. While your fingers are snapping, tap your feet in the same rhythm. Your movements have become more expressive. Begin to sway to the rhythm of the snaps and the taps. This is a kind of seated dance. Now all you need to do is stand and begin to move about to the snap-tap beat and you are certainly dancing.

If you take dance apart, you find it consists of just such body movements—a finger snap, a toe tap, a body sway, a step, a leap, all tied together with the rhythm of the music. If a song lyric is simply spoken dialogue built into a melodic, rhythmic pattern, a dance is simply body movements worked into a similar pattern.

The members of a school marching band do a kind of dance. When playing sports, athletes come close to dancing as they drive for a lay-up, race for a pass, stroke a tennis ball, run the hurdles. Gene Kelly gained fame as a dancer in musicals, although he once dreamed of playing shortstop for his hometown Pittsburgh Pirates. His dancing style does have an athletic flavor. On a

35

television program Kelly once demonstrated the relationship between athletic movements and dance. Professional athletes, including then Baltimore Colt all-star quarterback Johnny Unitas, demonstrated typical moves in their sports, such as throwing a pass. Kelly took each typical sports move and created a short dance sequence from it.

You don't march and you don't play sports? But do you ever move your hands about in an emotional conversation, expressing an idea with your hands? Add the beat of rhythm and you have a gesture dance.

Think about people plugged into personal stereo earphones, moving to the rhythm of the music they hear. They are dancing, dancing in their own musical world.

In theater musicals, everyday movements become the dance steps that tell a story, create a mood, or express a feeling.

Dance types:

You may have seen a movie starring Gene Kelly or Fred Astaire. Both dancers began their careers in Broadway musicals, then moved to Hollywood. When Astaire dances to the song "Top Hat" in the movie of that name, or when Kelly dances his classic sequence during "Singin' in the Rain" in that movie, each is dancing solo.

Solo dance

A solo dance expresses the performer's thoughts or feelings without uttering words. The soloist's movements can describe sadness, loneliness, triumph, joy, or fear.

Pas de deux (duet)

A duet involves two dancers, usually a man and a woman, or a boy and a girl. It is dialogue in movement. The song "Shall We Dance?" from *The King and I* has words, but more important are the stiff steps of the king as he begins to dance with his children's teacher. Then he gradually becomes more expressive as he realizes the pleasure of dancing with Anna.

Production number

The production number is to dance what the chorus is to song. Involving many dancers, it can establish the atmosphere of a scene, carnival, masquerade ball, circus, festival, or homecoming. Exciting to watch, it can give a story a kick in the pants after

36

a slow, serious moment, allowing the story's plot problems to stew before being resolved.

Because a production number involves many people dancing on a crowded stage, it requires precision and much practice. Some production numbers hardly seem like dancing and might not even have music, yet they still require planning and rehearsal.

As *Guys and Dolls* opens, you see a stage filled with police, chorus girls, gamblers, photographers, and tourists. As they move about, a street vendor rushes in pushing a baby buggy. He opens it and begins selling his goods. Spotting a policeman, the street salesman pulls down the buggy hood and nonchalantly walks past the officer. A tourist discovers his watch has been stolen. He chases the thief. The pickpocket, in turn, looks for the girl who has stolen it from him. The police officer begins trailing the street vendor and three gamblers, while the rest of the crowd continues milling about. It might appear as if everyone is moving haphazardly, but their bumping, running, ducking, frantic pace has been carefully planned and practiced so no stage accidents occur.

Ballet

A production number gives color and excitement to a musical production, but it adds little, if anything, to the plot. On the other hand, a ballet can tell a complete story by itself without words, only with the movements of the dancers. Great composers have created music for ballets that visually describe a story or theme with only dance. A ballet can include solo and duet sequences as well as a large group of dancers.

In 1938, Richard Rodgers and Lorenz Hart created the musical *On Your Toes*. The story involved a vaudeville dancer who gave up his popular career to dance classical ballet. For the story Rodgers composed "Slaughter on Tenth Avenue," a ballet pantomiming a New York killing. George Balanchine, America's foremost classical choreographer, designed the sequence, the first time a ballet was part of a musical.

"Slaughter on Tenth Avenue" had its own story and really had nothing to do with the plot of *On Your Toes*. When Rodgers joined Oscar Hammerstein II five years later to write *Oklahoma!*, they let a ballet tell part of their story. In the book plot Julie has a dream, which choreographer Agnes De Mille turned into a dance sequence. This time, ballet told part of the story, as it portrayed Julie's fears. Thereafter, many musicals used ballet to carry a segment of the book's plot.

Solo dances, duets, production numbers, and ballet can express the thoughts or feelings of a character, act as unspoken dialogue, or create atmosphere. Dance is an important part of the experience of a musical.

Question and Activities

Examining musicals

1. The snapping fingers of *West Side Story* suggest that you might create a gesture dance.

    a. Think of some gestures you use and apply a noun to them. Examples: snapping fingers (joy, pep), shrugging shoulders (bewilderment), thumbs up (success). Tell a story with gestures.

    b. Select some recorded music as background to your gesture story.

2. Act out some of the standard sports moves such as those suggested in this chapter: throwing a ball, swinging a bat, and so on. Select some song or piece of music that would fit the movements.

Listening to music

1. Listen to a recording of a musical that includes music for a dance sequence. Then decide how the dance music differs from the songs in the musical.

2. Study some video clips of pop-song dance presentations. Decide the following for each.

    a. What emotions does the dance project?

    b. Do those emotions fit the words of the song?

3. Now do the same for the dance of any videos of musicals you might be able to watch.

Creating a musical

1. If you are creating a class musical, decide which parts of the book plot lend themselves to dance interpretation. Describe the spirit such dances should take.

2. Exercises 1 and 2 under "Listening to music" on the previous page can help you choreograph dances for your musical. Here are the steps you might use:

   a. First decide what normal movements or gestures will fit the meaning or emotions of the dance.

   b. Exaggerate those movements as you work out a dance movement sequence.

   c. Choose some music that will fit the sequence.

   d. Relate the movement sequence to the music.

CHAPTER 7

Production

Richard D'Oyly Carte

presents

Gilbert & Sullivan's

» THE «

MIKADO

Fifth Avenue Theater

✳

The Mikado, like all Gilbert and Sullivan operettas, was directed by Gilbert himself. A meticulous worker, Gilbert spent months planning its staging with sketches and three-dimensional models, then instructed and rehearsed the performers until the production fitted his conception.

Richard D'Oyly Carte produced all Gilbert and Sullivan shows, even going so far as to build a theater, the Savoy, solely for the team's operettas. As producer he even had the task of keeping the two working together, for the writer and composer were hardly friends and for a period barely spoke to one another. Still, the shows went on.

A musical production is a single thing made up of several parts: the book, the lyrics, the music, and the dance. How do these parts come together? Through the work of:

the director, who manages the stage production, selecting and rehearsing the cast and pulling the music, dance, scenery, and lighting designs together into the finished production, and

the producer, who secures financial backing for the show, books the theater, hires the cast and orchestra, arranges for the costume and scenery acquisitions, publicizes the show, and handles all the business arrangements.

The book, lyrics, music, and choreography are nothing more than ideas hatched in the minds of the book's author, lyricist, composer, and choreographer. Until these are scrambled together and put into visual form by the production, they remain unrealized visions. Production turns imaginative ideas into visual reality.

Jesus Christ Superstar demonstrated how important production can be. Its one-season run in New York contrasted with its eight-year stay in London. Anthony Bowles, its London orchestra conductor, felt that the New York production was so lavish as to be in poor taste. Its simpler London staging better fitted its theme of the death of Jesus.

Casting:

When a musical goes into production, work begins for the whole company. The director must choose actors and actresses to play the parts of the characters described in the author's book. If the heroine is meant to be young, pretty, and sweet, an actress must be found to fit the part. If the heroine is supposed to be older, sexy, and brash, someone else must be hired.

Cast members must have the talent to meet the requirements of their roles. Singers are hired for those parts that stress singing, and other actors and actresses for the parts that have little singing. Comedians take the comic parts, and dancers, the dancing roles. Top performers can do it all.

A few performers have had all of these talents plus a dynamic stage personality. Such stars in a show means an exciting performance and, probably, box office success. Brassy, wide-eyed Carol Channing made a success of *Gentlemen Prefer Blondes* and *Hello, Dolly!*. Ethel Merman made *Gypsy, Call Me Madam, Annie Get Your Gun*, and many more box office hits.

Once the cast is set, rehearsals begin. Spoken parts are read and learned. The musical director coaches the singers, chorus, and orchestra. The choreographer instructs the dancers in the steps that he or she has designed.

The director oversees it all, making certain the dances, acting, and music all fit smoothly with one another. The performance must not confuse the plot; the message must come across clearly. The production must be visually appealing and musically delightful without kinks or cracks in its construction.

Design:

The cast rehearses in casual clothes on a bare stage. For the opening they will need scenery and costumes. Stage and costume design tie the show together in an attractive bundle.

What is the most unifying feature of the musical's book? It is the setting, the time and the place of the story. Stage scenery establishes the setting immediately, whether it is a nineteenth-century village or a twentieth-century city, a country lane, or an urban slum. The costumes tell you whether a character is a country bumpkin or a city slicker, a politician, pauper, or pusher.

Some songs introduced by Ethel Merman:

"I Get a Kick Out of You" (from Cole Porter's *Anything Goes*)

"Everything's Coming Up Roses" (from Jule Styne and Stephen Sondheim's *Gypsy*)

"It's a Lovely Day Today"

"You're Just in Love" (from Irving Berlin's *Call Me Madam*)

"They Say It's Wonderful"

"There's No Business Like Show Business" (from Irving Berlin's *Annie Get Your Gun*)

Scenery and costume design also support mood. Dimly lit scenes suggest threat. Brightly lit scenes give the atmosphere a lift. Vividly colored costumes prepared you for an upbeat experience. Dark costumes can introduce mystery or intrigue.

Scenic design

The stage designer who creates the scenery follows certain principles. First of all, a single design must serve several scenes. Musicals traditionally are divided into two acts. However, each act can include many scenes. *West Side Story* has fifteen scenes in two acts, *South Pacific* has twenty-four.

The visual difference between any two scenes may be slight, such as a change in the time of day. Yet, it may mean a change of location. Whether the change is large or not, the shift must occur without distraction.

Perhaps you have seen a play or musical in which performers act a scene in front of a closed curtain while a scene change is being made behind it. Unfortunately, the knocking about of stagehands who are moving scenery makes so much noise, you can hardly hear what is said in front of the curtain.

Careful planning prevents such problems. Some theaters have mechanically revolving stages, so that as one scene is being played in front of the audience, the next is being set up in the back. When the scene changes, the stage revolves, bringing the new scene before the audience.

Other theaters have elevator floors so that scenery prepared below the stage rises to replace a finished scene, sometimes before the marveling eyes of the audience. At other times, mechanisms lower scenery from above. All of these devices ease scene changes.

With revolving or elevating stages, precision planning for dance routines can be even more complicated. Kate Mostel, wife of Zero Mostel, the original Tevye in *Fiddler on the Roof,* tells of an incident that happened when she was one of the Rockettes (dancers) at New York's Radio City Music Hall. The stage was divided into three sections, each one operating as an elevator. Once, when the Rockettes stepped back onto one of the rising stages, a dancer was left behind and had to scramble after her slowly rising colleagues.

Many theaters are not so expensively equipped with elevators or revolving stages. Then directors must use simple devices to ease scene changes.

One method is to design a *unit set,* in which a single stage arrangement serves different scenes. Perhaps the inside of a house is shown on one side of the stage, a garden in the center, and a village street on the other side. When performers move from one side of the stage to the other, the scene changes.

Lighting is another effective way to make scene changes. Say the basic scenery is an outdoor setting. Stage lights darken, and a spotlight shines on a table and chairs. Just that easily, quickly, and quietly, the scene is now the corner of a room.

Scenic designers first sketch different views of a set to get an idea of how their concepts will look, then they choose the best. They often construct small models of their stage sets. This helps the director and choreographer better understand movement within the design. By studying a scale model, they might discover that some part of the set would get in the way of the performance. They can then have it changed before the scenery is built.

Costume design

Costumes help place the characters into the book's setting (time and place). They also help establish a character's personality, with a conservative dress for an innocent girl, overalls for a farmer, or vest, suit, and tie for a businessman. Costumes can do more than just identify personality. They can actually support the theme, as, for example, during the Ascot horse race scene in *My Fair Lady.*

This race is an annual aristocrat's bash in England. In the musical's setting of the race, all the women are formally dressed in black and white and the men in gray. When Eliza enters, she wears a pink gown and hat, setting her off from the rest. The warm, pink color of her dress gives her more life than the cold colors do for the others.

Then into the scene saunters Professor Higgins, dressed in his usual light-brown tweed suit and hat, poking fun at all the pomp. His costume, in marked contrast to the formal wear, makes visual mockery of the finery, just as his gibes make fun of the snobbery of Ascot.

Like the scenic designers, costume designers sketch out costume ideas. Costumes must fit the book's period and place setting. They must fit the roles of the characters. And, of course, they should make a visual impression. They also must not produce any technical performance problems. The medieval knights of the musical *Pippin* were required to wear armor. Because they also had to dance, the armor could not be stiff and heavy. The *Pippin* costume designer created armor of cheesecloth and latex covered by flexible metallic paint.

Out-of-town tryouts: Finally the musical is ready for presentation. For decades the out-of-town tryout was a traditional theater event. That generally meant a series of performances in theaters outside New York City. It is not as regular an occurrence today as it once was, for many of today's musicals have already been successfully staged in an off-Broadway theater before reaching a midtown Manhattan stage. The success of London musicals such as *The Phantom of the Opera* since the 1980's has meant they arrive in New York with their productions already in place.

Still, a completely new musical will have its production whipped into final shape away from New York, perhaps in Boston, Philadelphia, Chicago, or some other city. At the out-of-town tryout the director and producer see how audiences react to their presentation. They may discover in actual performance that a song does not go over or does not fit the sequence of the show's pacing. Then they drop the song and the composer writes a new one to replace it. Perhaps some lines fall flat or cause confusion in the story, and so must be rewritten. Maybe a joke gets no laughs, so it must be thrown out. If the show runs too long, it must be shortened. At the tryout everything is done to bring the musical as close to perfection as possible.

The 1925 musical *No No, Nanette* can give you an idea of the importance placed on the out-of-town tryout. Producer H. H. Frazee took the musical to the Midwest for its pre-New York run. Feeling uncomfortable with it, he delayed its Broadway opening in order to have the writers and composer rework it.

Moving around the Midwest, it spent eleven months alone in Chicago. Still unsure, Frazee sent it to London. Finally *No No, Nanette* reached New York, becoming a major musical of the 1920's and a major revival in 1971. It included a song written during the tryouts in place of a discarded number. The new song, "Tea for Two" became a pop classic.

Producing a musical, like brewing tea, brings together all the ingredients, then serves the brew for anyone who wishes to partake. If the tea leaves are tasty and the water pure, the lemon tart and the sugar sweet, then the musical brew will give a pleasant theatrical experience.

Exciting, entertaining theatrical experiences are what musicals are all about. The show begins with the author's book. Before it reaches the stage, many creative people become involved to bring the musical to life. We have seen how that happens. Now it is time to examine some of the most significant creations of the musical theater.

Questions and Activities

Examining music

1. Examine the stage of your school theater or gym and decide what equipment (curtains, lights, etc.) is available for student performances.

2. Casting is an important part of production. Discuss a movie or television show you have recently seen. Decide why major roles were given to each performer. In your opinion, was there any miscasting?

Listening to music

1. Listen to the recording of a musical. As an exercise, recast it by suggesting famous stars from the movies, television, or pop music world who you think would best play the parts and sing the roles.

Creating a musical

1. Will your class produce the musical you have been creating as an exercise? First divide the book of your musical into scenes— each a change of setting, time, or situation. Decide with which scene the second act should begin. The first act generally sets up the story problem and the second act resolves it. The second act is usually shorter than the first.

2. Beside a list of the scenes of your musical, write a description of how each scene should appear, including the props necessary for setting the scene. This is your scenic design. Keep it simple.

3. Draw costumes for each of the characters in your musical, or else photocopy or cut costume ideas from magazines or books.

4. Which students are interested in performing in your musical? When you have found out, assign parts according to the appearance and abilities of your cast.

Part II

Opening Night

Once the show has been written, the score composed, and the cast chosen and rehearsed, the project's most exciting moment arrives—the night on which the musical opens. Will it be a smashing hit or a bust? Judgment will come quickly, as the opening-night audience talks about the new musical during the intermission.

This second half of the book presents a decade-by-decade review of some of the triumphs of the American musical. Following each decade review are some thoughts for your own intermission talk. Now, the house lights dim, the overture begins and the curtain rises for...

OPENING NIGHT.

CHAPTER 8

Early Musical Theater

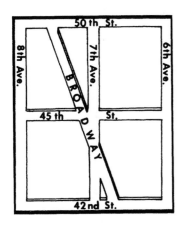

What do you imagine when you hear the name of the street called Broadway? You could see it on a map as a long avenue running south to north on New York's Manhattan Island. But most people think of it as the section where it angles across 42nd to 45th streets, carving out pie-shaped Times Square.

Today the theaters on Broadway compete with bars, cheap movies, traffic jams, and a touch of danger. However, the imagination can still paint the more mythical meaning of Broadway. Think of that same Times Square and the narrow streets leading into it filled with theaters such as the Ziegfeld, Winter Garden, and Majestic. Above their lighted entrances marquees proclaim their musical productions—*Show Boat, West Side Story,* or *The Music Man.* Because of such theaters the name Broadway is synonymous with the phrase "American musical theater."

There is no particular date from which to begin examining the development of musicals. However, Gilbert and Sullivan's English operettas are as convenient a place to start as any. Their operettas had the biting satire and rich humor that American musicals would adopt and develop. Gilbert and Sullivan shows were very popular in America, each enjoying a long American run after arriving from London. The first had been *H.M.S. Pinafore,* which opened in Boston on November 25, 1878. That was followed by *The Pirates of Penzance,* then *The Mikado* in 1885.

In the decade that followed, musical theater meant either Gilbert and Sullivan or close imitations. Then, in 1894, another British import, *A Gaiety Girl,* opened in New York. One of the first shows to be called **musical comedy,** it used the pop song styles of the day rather than European waltzes for its score. It also relied more on comic plot situations than witty songs for its comedy.

As the nineteenth century ended, home-bred musicals employed the pop tune flavor of *A Gaiety Girl*. Farfetched fantasy in exotic lands drove the book plots of many of those early musicals, even when the exotic setting was no more foreign than San Francisco's Chinatown.

Book by Charles H. Hoyt
Music by Percy Gaunt
Starring J. Aldrich Libby and Loie Fuller

Charles Hoyt had already written a number of musicals when *A Trip to Chinatown* opened in 1890 at his Madison Square Theater in New York. It ran for 657 performances, a record for nineteenth-century musicals. As in most early musicals, the songs and dances had little relation to the story. The show drew audiences happy to hear its songs, including one which had nothing to do with Chinatown, San Francisco, or even California. Instead, it sang of "The Bowery" in New York City.

The show also included "After the Ball." Its composer, Charles K. Harris, paid Hoyt $500 to have it sung in the musical. The trick worked, as "After the Ball" then sold a record 5 million copies of sheet music.

| "The Bowery" |
| "Reuben and Cynthia" |
| "After the Ball" |

> *Book:* A young man goes to the restaurant in Chinatown where his uncle is expecting to meet the young man's date. The young couple avoids the uncle and the waiters, who are after the nephew's empty wallet, by sneaking from dining room to dining room in the restaurant. All ends well when the forgiving uncle pays the bill and all hard feelings are forgotten.

As the twentieth century began, musicals continued the formula of mixing popular songs with stories. Typical was *In Dahomey*, which opened on February 18, 1903. The show was atypical in that it was the first all African-American musical to play in a major New York theater.

Book by Jesse A. Ship
Music by Paul Laurence Dunbar and Alex Rogers
Music by Will Marion Cook
Starring Bert Williams and George Walker

> *Book:* The Boston-based Get-the-coin Syndicate plans to colonize Africa with poor American blacks. Their representatives Rareback Pinkerton and Shylock Homestead head for Florida to con an elderly rich man out of his fortune. When Rareback discovers that Shylock has even more money than their intended victim, he turns to hustling his partner and is soon sporting about Florida and Dahomey in the latest flashy fashions. Although both become governors, their inauguration celebrated with lively African dancing,

Rareback's high-handed swindling turn Shylock against him and the two have a falling-out.

Williams and Walker had formed a vaudeville team that became popular in West Coast theaters. Moving east, Bert Williams became a legend as one of the country's leading comedians. *In Dahomey* was built around the routines of the two performers and the lyrics of Paul Laurence Dunbar, a major African-American poet and novelist. The songs included "Broadway in Dahomey," which is sung when Rareback and Shylock take their American hustle to Africa. Social attitudes in 1903 limited *In Dahomey* to 53 New York performances. In London, the musical had a respectable seven-month run.

The following year saw musical theater's first superstar score a Broadway hit. George M. Cohan, an all-around performer as actor, singer, and dancer, created the book, music, and lyrics for his shows. He then directed them as well, usually including family members in the cast. His flag-waving, sentimental poetry and unsophisticated melodies have dated much of Cohan's works. Yet many of his songs have remained standards, including one he wrote for *Little Johnny Jones* in 1904, "Give My Regards to Broadway." No wonder a statue of George M. Cohan stands on Broadway at Times Square.

Book, lyrics, and music by George M. Cohan
Starring George M. Cohan, Ethel Levey, and Tom Lewis

Book: *American jockey Johnny Jones arrives in England to ride in the Derby. When Johnny's horse loses, bookie Anthony Anstey spreads the word that Jones threw the race. Facing an angry crowd as he is about to leave England, Johnny vows to remain until a detective clears his name of the frame-up. As his ship sails without him, Johnny asks his friends on board to "Give My Regards to Broadway." In time the ship returns with the news that Johnny has been cleared. However, Anstey has kidnapped Johnny's girl Goldie Gate (played by Cohan's wife Ethel Levey). Johnny traces them to San Francisco, where Anstey manages a casino. Thinking that "Life's a Funny Proposition" as he searches through the colorful confusion of Chinatown, Johnny locates the casino and rescues Goldie.*

"The Yankee Doodle Boy"

"Give My Regards to Broadway"

"Life's a Funny Proposition After All"

Musical comedies such as *In Dahomey* and *Little Johnny Jones* were not the only kinds of musical entertainment in the years before World War I. Two other types were to have an impact on musical theater. They were revues and operettas.

The revue: The word **revue** might make you think of the other word pronounced in the same way—review. However, the theater word is French, derived from a kind of Parisian entertainment featuring

51

music, variety acts, comedy sketches, and lots of pretty chorus girls. A sideshow manager from the Midwest named Florenz Ziegfeld visited Paris and fell in love with French *revue* and a showgirl named Anna Held. He brought both back to the United States.

Such variety entertainment was not new to American theaters. Minstrel shows had offered comedy and songs. Vaudeville sent variety shows touring the country. Burlesque offered parody acts and low comedy as well as pretty women in corsets and tights. Ziegfeld's shows were similar, but he added class to variety, using the French word to proclaim his taste.

He called his revue the *Ziegfeld Follies*, and staged the first in 1907. Each year Ziegfeld presented a new edition, continuing until he died in 1932. Each new production was more magnificent than the previous as he offered glamour, excitement, first-rate material, and decency to attract the entire family. But most of all he offered spectacle, such as the final number of the first act of the *Ziegfeld Follies* of 1927. All members of the cast, including the huge chorus wearing white satin decorated with yellow fringe, posed on a stage-wide, semicircular staircase while two orchestras with fourteen pianos played from those same steps.

The *Ziegfeld Follies* were not musicals in the strictest sense of the word. However, some of the stars of musicals got their start in, or appeared in, the *Follies* or other revues. More important, composers of musicals often began their careers with revue productions. George Gershwin wrote many songs for *George White's Scandals*, a rival revue to Ziegfeld's. Richard Rodgers and Lorenz Hart's first complete work was for a revue entitled *The Garrick Gaieties* (`gay-it-ees). Irving Berlin and Cole Porter composed for revues, as did Victor Herbert and Jerome Kern.

American operetta: Victor Herbert was born in Ireland and studied music in Germany and Vienna. Classically trained, he arrived in New York to become the country's foremost composer by the beginning of the century. His musical outlet was mainly in operetta, including *Babes in Toyland, Naughty Marietta, The Red Mill,* and *Mlle. Modiste.* Some of them continue to be revived.

Herbert's music raised American operetta to the level of Europe's best. More importantly, his compositions lifted theatrical musical taste just as Ziegfeld's *Follies* raised production taste. "Ah, Sweet Mystery of Life," "Sweethearts," "A Kiss in the Dark," and "Kiss Me Again" are just some of Herbert's songs that have survived. Romantic, lilting, with rich harmony and sweeping melody, his songs raised all the sound colors of a full orchestra.

The book plots of Herbert's operettas did little more than give him story situations on which to hang his songs. In Chapter 4 we saw how Herbert composed the music for "Kiss Me Again," then left it for his lyricist Henry Blossom to write words so it would fit into their operetta *Mlle. Modiste*.

Book and lyrics by Henry Blossom
Music by Victor Herbert
Starring Fritzi Scheff and Walter Percival

"If I Were on the Stage"

"Kiss Me Again"

"The Time and the Place and the Girl"

"What I Want When I Want It"

Book: Fifi, a salesgirl in a Paris hat shop, hopes to become a singer. She is also in love with Captain Etienne de Bourvray. However, the hat shop owner's son is expecting to marry Fifi. Making the situation more difficult is Etienne's uncle, who forbids the captain to marry an ordinary shop clerk. An open-spirited American meets Fifi and agrees to pay for her music studies. Time passes until Etienne's uncle hosts a charity party on his estate. Fifi, known now as Madame Bellini, sings at the affair. The uncle is so impressed with her talent and manner that he withdraws his objections to the marriage and all ends happily.

VERY
GOOD,
EDDIE

Until World War I Victor Herbert was the major musical force in American theater. Then, in 1917, he composed the music for three new shows. All three flopped. But a young composer named Jerome Kern was enjoying success with *Oh, Boy!*, *Leave It to Jane*, and *Very Good, Eddie*. Listening to Kern's music and watching his success, Herbert said that the new composer would inherit his position in the musical theater.

However, Kern would not adopt Herbert's approach to composing for the theater. Kern felt the most important element of a musical was the book. It was the book that tied everything together. All else grew out of the book. That attitude changed the direction of the American musical.

Prior to Kern, most theater music was written to please the audience, not to fit a story plot. Comedians jumped into the plot to deliver their popular comic routines. Chorus girls danced into the plot to prance their prettiest. All these baubles were simply strung on the slender thread of a book plot.

Kern believed that the humor should come from the book's comic situations. The wit of the songs should develop out of the book's dialogue. It did not hurt that Kern's writers were Guy Bolton and P. G. Wodehouse. Their sophisticated humor and writing gave Kern the solid book to inspire his compositions. Jerome Kern would make a major contribution to musicals in the decade of the 1920's.

The American musical received its first nurturing from British imports. Revue and operetta added nourishment to its adolescent musical attempts. By the 1920's it was ready to develop into a new type of theatrical creation.

Questions and Activities

Examining musicals

1. Are the names of any of the songs, shows, composers, writers, or performers mentioned in this chapter familiar to you?

2. Is there any form of entertainment today in the movies, on television, or in the theater that resembles revue?

3. Why do some shows seem fresh and exciting years after they were first presented, while most shows become dated in time?

4. Discuss how Kern's approach to creating musicals brought about a maturing of American musicals.

5. One of Kern's writers was P. G. Wodehouse. If you read one of Wodehouse's books about Jeeves the butler, you will discover the good fun and light wit that made Kern's early musicals successful. Those books are available in libraries and as paperbacks.

Listening to music

1. Although it may be difficult to find recordings of entire Victor Herbert shows, it is not hard to find recordings of his music. Most of those songs will have come from his operettas, often performed as concert music without the words. Listen to some to get a feeling for the rich melody of Herbert's compositions.

Creating a musical

Your class may have decided to learn more about musicals by trying to create one. The first half of the book presented ideas on how that might be done. This second half suggests a book idea for you—a musical about the history of musicals. Such a musical might follow the career of a Broadway star. Each scene could depict another decade in the performer's life.

Act I, Scene *i*:

Our star performs as a child singer in a Broadway theater sometime in the first two decades of the twentieth century.

1. Write a scene for this part of the star's life.
2. Which songs from this period would you choose for this scene?
3. Draw or photocopy examples of period costumes that could be used in this first scene.

Reading the critics

What does the comment in *The New York Times* mentioning the opening of *In Dahomey* tell you about social attitudes in the first decade of the twentieth century?

CHAPTER 9

The 1920's

History has dubbed the 1920's the Jazz Age because this new music fit the spirit of prohibition, silent movies, and the free-living style of the decade. Jazz arrived in time to set a new tempo for musicals, turning them into something different from operetta. When show dancing was paced to a jazz beat, another special feature was added.

Both first bounded onto a musical stage in 1920 with *Shuffle Along*. As one critic wrote, with that musical, "all stage dancing underwent a change, steps became more intricate, daring, perilous."

Book and lyrics by Eubie Blake and Noble Sissle
Music by Eubie Blake
Starring Noble Sissle, Florence Mills, F. E. Miller,
  and Aubrey Lyles

Singer Noble Sissle and Harlem jazz pianist Eubie Blake joined the comedy-dancing pair Flourney E. Miller and Aubrey Lyles to create *Shuffle Along*. Harlem loved the musical, but it could get no other New York booking. The show toured New Jersey and Pennsylvania, then returned to New York to open at the 63rd Street Music Hall. Although it had not reached the theater district, Broadway's fans found *Shuffle Along*. The police had to turn 63rd Street into a one-way street to handle the traffic flocking to the musical. It ran for 504 performances in New York, a strong showing for the 1920's, then toured the country with two companies until 1924.

However, more important than its performance tally was its ground-breaking role in forming the American musical. The staging energy and excitement of *Shuffle Along* became the distinguishing feature of musicals ever after.

"I'm Just Wild About Harry"

"Bandana Days"

"Love Will Find a Way"

Book: *Three candidates are running for mayor of Jimtown. Two of them, crooked business partners, promise one another they will appoint the losing partner chief of police. When the third, a reform candidate, loses, the new mayor and police chief begin cashing in on their positions. The reform politician then becomes active and manages to unseat the two scoundrels.*

Book by Guy Bolton and Fred Thomson
Lyrics by Ira Gershwin
Music by George Gershwin
Starring Fred Astaire, Adele Astaire, Cliff Edwards

Lady, Be Good!, opening on December 1, 1924, united two brothers for their first theatrical collaboration. Ira Gershwin had already written words for some of his brother George's songs, but this was their first musical together.

"Fascinating Rhythm"

"Lady, Be Good"

"Oh What a Lovely Party"

"So Am I"

Book: *Brother and sister Dick and Susie Trevor are a dance team down on their luck. Because Dick has rejected the flirting of their landlady, wealthy Josephine Vanderwater, she has evicted them from their home. Dick's lawyer Watty Watkins tries getting the three to make up. His fee? He wants Susie to impersonate a Mexican woman who has been jailed for biting a man's ear. If freed, she will inherit her late husband's fortune. However, the husband is not actually dead but is a tramp whom Susie has befriended. The "tramp," who is wealthy, proves that his marriage to the ear-nipping Mexican was illegally forced upon him. Therefore, he is free to marry Susie. His fortunes restored, the tramp helps Dick free himself from Miss Vanderwater in order to marry Shirley, his true love.*

A scheming rich woman and an unemployed dance team saved by a wealthy tramp may seem like a farfetched plot, yet *Lady, Be Good!* was a success. It had the music of the Gershwins, a great song in "Fascinating Rhythm," and the exciting dancing of the Astaires.

"Best musical in town."
—*The World*

In the 1920's Fred and Adele Astaire performed dance acts in revues and had minor roles in a few musicals. A natural song for the Astaires was "Fascinating Rhythm." One is struck by its upbeat tempo and the changing rhythms Gershwin worked into it. This was ideal for the rapid-fire steps alternating with grace that was the Fred Astaire style.

Astaire always worked hard to make a dance routine work perfectly, but somehow he had difficulty fashioning a satisfactory conclusion to "Fascinating Rhythm." It may come as a surprise to learn that it was the composer George Gershwin who created the steps with which Astaire closed the number. In short, music, lyrics, song, and dance all came together when the Gershwins and Astaires combined to create *Lady, Be Good!*, a classic musical.

Another important work premiered the night after *Lady, Be Good!* opened. It was *The Student Prince*, an operetta that opened at the Jolson Theater on December 2, 1924.

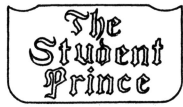

Book and lyrics by Dorothy Donnelly
Music by Sigmund Romberg
Starring Howard Marsh and Ilse Marvenga

Dorothy Donnelly based her book on a long-running play entitled *Old Heidelberg*. As *The Student Prince*, the adaptation continued the operetta tradition into the 1920's. It was the logical style for the composer Sigmund Romberg. Operettas had originated in Central Europe and it was there, in Hungary, that Romberg had grown up before coming to the United States. *The Student Prince* was not Romberg's only work, but it was perhaps his most successful.

"Students' Marching Song"

"Drinking Song"

"Deep in My Heart, Dear"

"Serenade"

"Nevermore"

Book: *Prince Karl Franz arrives at the University of Heidelberg with his tutor, both disguised in order that the prince might live the life of an ordinary student. At the Inn of the Three Golden Apples they are joined by other male students singing the stirring "Students' Marching Song." That is followed by an equally rousing "Drinking Song." The prince falls in love with the inn's waitress Kathie and together they sing "Deep in My Heart, Dear." He further swears his love with a "Serenade." When the prince's grandfather falls ill, Karl Franz must leave Heidelberg to assume his royal duties, which also means he must marry royalty. He returns one last time to Heidelberg to see Kathie and admit that, although he will never forget her, he will see her "Nevermore."*

"People don't like sad musicals!" complained Lee Schubert, one of the brothers producing the Romberg-Donnelly operetta. And where were the chorus girls? It would never work. It had to be changed.

Donnelly and Romberg would not change the story, and even threatened legal action if the musical were not produced as written. The Shuberts relented. *The Student Prince* lasted for 608 performances, a long run in the 1920's. Even as it played in New York, nine companies toured the country giving performances that would continue for another quarter of a century. It was so popular it became a movie while films were still silent. The movie theater pianist played its songs, but a silent musical still may be difficult to imagine. In 1954 *The Student Prince* became a sound movie with Mario Lanza singing the songs of Prince Karl Franz. It is now a permanent fixture as an American operetta.

Book by Otto Harbach and Frank Mandel
Lyrics by Irving Caesar and Otto Harbach
Music by Vincent Youmans
Starring Louise Groody and Charles Winninger

Sigmund Romberg did not change *The Student Prince* and it succeeded. Vincent Youmans spent a year changing *No No, Nanette* and it succeeded. There are no strict rules in the theater business. Chapter 7 described this show's tortuous, year-long, pre-New York tour. Two songs composed during the try-out rewrites, "I Want to Be Happy" and "Tea for Two," became the hits of the show when it arrived in New York on September 16, 1925.

Book: Billy Early, a Bible publisher, spends his profits on pretty young women, to the despair of his wife. At the same time, his rebellious daughter Nanette worries him with her own flings and flirts. When Nanette flashes her eyes at her father's lawyer, her boyfriend Tom reacts in desperation. The events and people in the show all come together in Atlantic City. Tom paints a charming picture of domestic bliss and tea for only two, meaning Nannette and himself. She does not like the quaint picture. Then her mother, Mrs. Early, shows up. Out go her husband's girlfriends. Dashed are the lawyer's hopes for Nanette. Together come Tom and Nanette. And Mrs. Early begins to enjoy her husband's Bible business profits. The audience gets a happy ending this time along with good songs, plenty of comedy, and carefree entertainment.

"Tea for Two"

"I Want To Be Happy"

SHOW BOAT

Book and lyrics by Oscar Hammerstein II
Music by Jerome Kern
Starring Charles Winninger, Howard Marsh, Helen Morgan, and Jules Bledsoe

The musicals of the 1920's that we have looked at so far seem to fit a pattern of fairy tale unreality with a prince, flirtations, old Europe, glossy Atlantic City, pure young love, and light plots. Now read the story told by *Show Boat*, which opened on December 27, 1927.

"Make Believe"

"You Are Love"

"Why Do I Love You?"

"Ol' Man River"

"Can't Help Lovin' Dat Man"

Book: The time is the 1880's. A show boat called the Cotton Blossom *docks at Natchez. Its star is singer Julie la Verne, performing along with her husband Steve as the show's main act. Attending the evening performance, gambler Gaylord Ravenal falls in love with Magnolia, daughter of the show boat's captain. Singing "Make Believe," Magnolia realizes she loves Gaylord. However, the local sheriff suggests that Gaylord leave town because of his gambling reputation. Before the* Cotton Blossom *itself departs, the sheriff returns, this time revealing that Julie is part black. Steve is white. To pacify local prejudice, Julie and Steve leave the show and Magnolia replaces her. Gaylord, still hanging about, takes over Steve's role.*

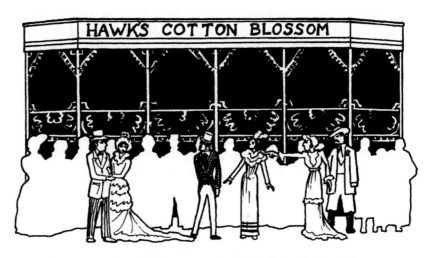

HAWKS COTTON BLOSSOM

A decade later at the 1893 Chicago World's Fair, Gaylord abandons Magnolia and their small child, because of his unbearable gambling debts. In order to survive, Magnolia looks for a singing job. One possibility is to replace an alcoholic singer—who turns out to be Julie, so changed that Magnolia does not recognize her. However, Julie understands Magnolia and her situation, so she gives up her job for the young mother. Although she becomes a star, Magnolia answers her father's plea to return to the Cotton Blossom. *More time passes until the 1920's, when Gaylord again appears. Even though their daughter has grown and their young years are long gone, the two reunite on board the show boat.*

Compared with most earlier book plots, this story has more depth, dealing with profound human problems. When Oscar Hammerstein II and Jerome Kern decided to adapt this story for the musical stage, they faced two obstacles. First, they needed Edna Ferber's permission to adapt her novel of the same name. Only when Kern convinced her he was thinking of a new type of musical, one which could tell a serious story, did the famous writer consent.

The pair's second problem was just the reverse. They had to convince producer Florenz Ziegfeld that such a serious story could have audience appeal and become a successful musical. Once committed, Ziegfeld backed them with his usual elaborate production. The *Show Boat* audience saw the busy dockside as the *Cotton Blossom* landed, looked on as Julie sang in the boat's interior theater, and then, in the second act, attended the Chicago World's Fair.

Show Boat marked a new direction for American musicals. First of all, it deals with realistic characters and their problems. It is not the imaginative, light farce of typical musicals. The issues—addiction, for example—are serious. Julie is an alcoholic and

"It is daring in its originality and shows that managers have not until now realized the tremendous possibilities of the musical comedy as an art form. It is a work of genius."

—Robert Coleman,
New York Daily Mirror

Gaylord a compulsive gambler. And then there are race relations. Julie and her boyfriend must leave the *Cotton Blossom* because of racial bigotry. A dramatic moment occurs when Julie's boyfriend Steve cuts her finger in front of the sheriff and then sucks her blood to show that he would become part black like her if he could. But this action is of no use; racial prejudice allows little room for symbolism. Joe, the dockhand, suffers the economic trap in which blacks labored. When he can find no fair or just reason why his work should be so back-breaking and his life so unpromising, he can do nothing but ask "Ol' Man River," for there *is* no fair or just answer.

Hammerstein fashioned Joe's song after traditional spirituals. He used the river as a symbol, as did some early African-American songs such as "Deep River," "Roll, Jordon Roll," and "Wade in the Water."

"Ol' Man River" was sung in the original production by Jules Bledsoe, then in the 1928 and 1932 stagings and 1935 film by Paul Robeson. It has become an American classic. When William Warfield sang it in the 1950's movie version, there were film theaters in which the audience actually applauded and the film was stopped and rewound so they could hear the song again.

The final test of any musical is the music. Kern and Hammerstein created magnificent songs, some of the best either ever wrote. There were love songs—"Make Believe," "You Are Love," and "Why Do I Love You?"—as well as Julie's torch songs, "Can't Help Lovin' Dat Man" and "Bill," which became song standards.

The two creators *wove* these songs into the story plot, not merely added them to kick up its pace. The songs helped establish the personalities and relationships of the characters. All of these features—

1. serious story with real people and problems
2. songs that carried the story line
3. marvelous music

—made Hammerstein and Kern's *Show Boat* a high point in the development of the American musical.

Movie Musicals

Two months before *Show Boat* opened, an event occurred that would soon affect musical entertainment. It was the showing of *The Jazz Singer*, the first major movie with sound. Although the only sound the movie theater audience heard was the singing of Al Jolson, the star, it was not a musical in the true sense. Except for those songs and a few brief bits of dialogue, the film was silent.

None of the film's songs were new. Instead, they were songs Jolson had already made popular on the stage. "Toot Toot Tootsie, Goodbye" and "My Gal Sal" were two of them. Jolson, in his minstrel show blackface, also got down on bent knee and sang his best known song, "Mammy." The songs had nothing to do with the plot. Nor were there other forms of music or dance. *The Jazz Singer* was not a musical. But with the coming of sound, Hollywood could get into the musical-making business.

Screenplay by Norman Houston and James Gleason
Songs by Arthur Freed and Nacio Herb Brown
Starring Bessie Love and Charles King

Two years passed before Hollywood released an original musical. Titled *The Broadway Melody*, it acknowledged the capital of musical theater. However, the songs were created for Hollywood. This was the first score ever composed solely for the screen.

> ***Screenplay:*** *In this typical Broadway theater plot, a musical star, played by Bessie Love, loses her performing partner as well as the man she loves because of her stage ambitions.*

If its story line was thin, the movie's songs were solid, something that would be true of many Hollywood musicals. The film's numbers included the title song as well as "The Wedding of the Painted Doll" and "You Were Meant for Me," both of which will appear again later in our story.

In two ways the American musical tradition blossomed in full in the 1920's. An original American creation, the movie musical, made its debut. And when the *Cotton Blossom* docked on its New York stage, *Show Boat* proved that songs could join the plot of a serious story to create a successful musical production.

Questions and Activities

Examining musicals

1. What songs, shows, or performers mentioned in this chapter about the 1920's were already familiar to you?

2. Can you explain why the song "In Dahomey" would be appropriate for the score for *Show Boat*?

3. Considering the eventual success of both *Show Boat* and *The Student Prince*, why were producers reluctant to back them?

Listening to music

1. There are many recordings of songs from both *The Student Prince* and *Show Boat*. Listen to and compare some of their songs.

   a. Which songs in *Show Boat* could be considered similar to the operetta style of those in *The Student Prince*?

   b. Discuss how the style of other *Show Boat* songs, such as "Life Upon the Wicked Stage" and "Bill," differs from operetta style.

2. Many Gershwin songs that have become pop standards were originally composed for stage musicals and later movie musicals. Besides those mentioned for *Lady, Be Good!* in this chapter, here are some more: "The Man I Love" (written for *Lady, Be Good!* but dropped, only to become popular in its own right), "Love Is Here to Stay," "But Not for Me," "Someone to Watch Over Me," "They Can't Take That Away From Me," "I Got Rhythm," and "Stairway to Paradise." If you can't hear songs from *Lady, Be Good!*, look for these.

Creating a musical

Act I, Scene *ii*:

In the 1920's, the star of our musical history becomes a dancer in a Broadway musical.

1. Expand the book plot by depicting the excitement and disappointments of attaining success on Broadway.

2. Create some dance steps or suggest a popular dance of the 1920's for this young dancing star.

3. Which songs of the decade will be sung in this scene?

4. Design costumes and props for this scene.

Reading the critics

Discuss why Robert Coleman used the words "daring," "originality," and "art form" in his *Daily Mirror* review of *Show Boat*.

CHAPTER 10

The 1930's

What picture does your imagination paint of America in the 1930's, the Depression years? Long lines of people looking for work? Soup lines with people waiting for charity food? There is another line—people standing to buy tickets for a movie. Seeking inexpensive escape from the hard times of the 1930's, Americans found it packaged by Hollywood. In a darkened movie theater people could forget that the store was in the red, the job was gone, or the farm was about to be repossessed. Fantasy was the escape, so Hollywood answered with visions more fantastic than ordinary imaginations could dream up.

Have you ever seen a movie musical from the Depression years? They are spectacular, with chorus dancers parading up and down wide staircases, wearing huge feathered hairpieces and spangled gowns. Today, most of those musicals appear gaudy and corny. Yet a few of them are still shown, especially if they feature dancing legend Fred Astaire and his partner Ginger Rogers.

Screenplay by Dwight Taylor and Allan Scott
Score by Irving Berlin
Starring Fred Astaire and Ginger Rogers

Fred Astaire had starred in such Broadway musicals as *Lady, Be Good!* and *Funny Face* with his sister Adele as partner. After Adele's marriage, Fred Astaire moved to Hollywood and got a new partner, Ginger Rogers. They first appeared together in *Flying Down to Rio* in 1933, and they earned top billing in *Top Hat*.

Screenplay: *The plot of* Top Hat *is simple enough. Jerry Travers (Fred Astaire) falls in love with Dale Tremont (Ginger Rogers). She mistakenly believes Jerry is married to a friend of hers. Actually, her friend's husband is a close friend of Jerry. Dancing and romancing, Jerry eventually convinces Dale he is free and in love with her.*

"Top Hat"

"No Strings"

"Dancing Cheek to Cheek"

What makes *Top Hat* important are the songs by Irving Berlin and the dancing of Astaire and Rogers. One waits through the silly misunderstandings and frothy comedy for the dances, then settles back for minutes of musical and visual delight. Astaire begins with his first solo, "No Strings." He dances the title song with a chorus of male dancers, all in "Top Hat," white tie, and tails. Then, dancing "Cheek To Cheek," Rogers and Astaire display the sophistication, high style, and perfection that made their art the model by which all musical duet dancing since has been measured.

Book by Guy Bolton and P. G. Wodehouse; revised by Howard Lindsay and Russel Crouse
Lyrics and music by Cole Porter
Starring Ethel Merman, William Gaxton, and Victor Moore

Despite having stars like Astaire and Rogers, Hollywood could not rival the originality, songs, and spirit of Broadway's stage musicals. In keeping with Depression escapism, Cole Porter's *Anything Goes* took place on an ocean liner. However, its voyage to the stage was a choppy one.

The original plot involved a group of shipwrecked passengers. When the liner *Morro Castle* burned near the New Jersey coast, good taste suggested the show's shipwreck plot should be wrecked and another substituted. The original writers were unavailable, and Russel Crouse was introduced to the show's director Howard Lindsay to collaborate on the rewrite. It became a partnership that would produce many Broadway productions in the years to come.

"So popular are Porter's lyrics that it is now considered the smart thing to know them all by heart, to rattle them off loudly."

—*Time*

More rough water occurred when the child of famed pilot Charles Lindbergh was kidnapped, then found dead. Respecting the parents' tragedy, Porter dropped a line from his song "You're the Top" that mentioned Mrs. Lindbergh. Once such references to tragic news were dropped from the story, *Anything Goes* set sail on November 21, 1934, at the Alvin Theater.

"I Get a Kick Out of You"

"You're the Top"

"Blow, Gabriel, Blow"

"All Through the Night"

Book: *The plot of* Anything Goes *remained on board ship but without any sinking. Before sailing, woman evangelist Reno Sweeney claims to Billy Crocker that "I Get a Kick Out of You." As in many plots, her hero loves another, Hope Harcourt. Hope, in turn, plans to marry a rich aristocrat when the boat docks in Europe. Hope and Reno have tickets for the voyage. Billy, without a ticket, stows away. Using various disguises to escape detection, Billy finally manages to get a ticket and passport from the Reverend Dr. Moon, a fugitive scoundrel. While the ship is still at sea, word is received that Dr. Moon is no longer sought by the police and that a business deal has relieved Hope of needing to marry the*

"'You're the Top' is the most exciting lyric ever composed for a song."

—*New York Sun-Record*

You're The Top!

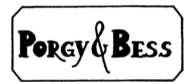

"...TER-IFffff–IC-LY, yet
I get a kick out of you!"

aristocrat. Hope marries Billy, so Reno and the jilted aristocrat pair off and all ends conveniently well.

Music and performance turned the contrived plot of *Anything Goes* into a historical musical moment. Playing the evangelist Reno Sweeney, Ethel Merman flashed on as a Broadway star who would shine for decades. "She knocked the audience, totally unprepared, for a loop," commented Russel Crouse, describing how Merman opened the show with an explosion by singing Porter's "I Get a Kick Out of You."

It is unusual for such a blockbuster song to begin a show, but there it was in *Anything Goes*. Merman ignited the blockbuster by breaking the word "terrifically" in the middle, holding the phrase until her breath gave out, then driving on through the rest of the word and song.

Porter composed songs of various styles, once again demonstrating how variety paces a show. "Blow, Gabriel, Blow" had all the power of a gospel song. "You're the Top" bounced as a snappy jump tune. "All Through the Night" smoldered as a smoking love song. Cole Porter was a master of witty lyrics as well as a sophisticated maker of melodies. *Anything Goes* not only proved that claim but turned out to be one of his finest musicals.

PORGY & BESS

Libretto by Du Bose Heyward
Lyrics by Ira Gershwin and Du Bose Heyward
Music by George Gershwin
Starring Todd Duncan, Anne Browne, and John W. Bubbles

When is a musical a musical and when is it not? That question bothers people trying to define *Porgy and Bess*. You have already met George Gershwin as the composer of *Lady, Be Good!* With the lyrics supplied by his brother Ira, George created other important Broadway shows. Therefore, *Porgy and Bess* might be expected to be a musical.

The problem is, it employs music and singing for dialogue, not just for songs. This is an opera tradition. That is why the sung book is called a **libretto**, an opera term. The theme is serious, involving drug addiction and murder, with very little comic relief. Therefore, *Porgy and Bess* could be considered an opera.

Little of the music is in classical opera form, however. Instead, Gershwin employed jazz, gospel, and pop sounds along with more traditional song. To the rescue of classifying it comes another term to describe *Porgy and Bess*—American folk opera. Now, leave terms aside and simply enjoy this work as a high point in the history of the American musical theater.

Book: *It is midsummer, which you learn as the curtain rises upon a young mother singing a "Summertime" lullaby to her baby. Their home is a waterfront ghetto of Charleston, South Carolina, called Catfish Row. Here lives the crippled beggar Porgy, who gets about on a goat-drawn cart. Although he has nothing but a poor shack and his goat cart, that nothing is enough for Porgy as he sings "I Got Plenty o' Nuttin'." Porgy has offered refuge to drug addict Bess, who is hiding out from the law.*

Recognizing his faith and goodness, Bess comes to love Porgy as he loves her. Then into their lives pushes her ex-boyfriend Crown, a huge bully who terrorizes the inhabitants of Catfish Row. After Crown is killed in a fight, Porgy is arrested on suspicion of murder. While he is absent, the dealer Sportin' Life tempts Bess with drugs. Giving in to the temptation, Bess flees with Sportin' Life to New York. Porgy, freed, returns home to plead, "Bess, Oh Where's My Bess?" Told the truth of her flight, Porgy demands his goat cart be hitched up. The people of Catfish Row argue that New York is too far for a poor goat. "Get my goat!" orders Porgy and as the curtain descends, sets off singing, "Oh Lawd, I'm On My Way."

Poverty, drugs, violence, and ghetto life serve as the ingredients of this story plot. *Porgy and Bess* demonstrated how serious stories could be joined to music, as had *Show Boat* a decade earlier. Both works include realities of the African-American experience. And the production's opening number, "Summertime," joined "Ol' Man River" as an American classic. Both are performed in concert as well as on the theater stage.

A crippled street beggar whom writer Du Bose Heyward frequently encountered inspired him to create the novel *Porgy*. Then, with Dorothy Heyward, he adapted the novel as a play. The story of Porgy did not end there, as the play haunted Gershwin with the idea of basing a musical work on the tale.

After opening in Boston on September 30, 1935, then moving on to New York on October 10, *Porgy and Bess* suffered at the hands of critics and lasted for only 124 performances. It was George Gershwin's last major work, for he died two years later, not yet forty years of age.

But *Porgy and Bess* survived. In 1942 a new production was mounted. It ran in New York for two seasons, then toured for a longer period. In 1952 *Porgy and Bess* was staged once more, this time in Dallas. That production toured the United States and then Europe, playing in major opera houses, theaters, and music festivals. A year later it returned to the United States, this time to enjoy a long New York run, before once more touring. Soon after, Hollywood made a film version of *Porgy and Bess*. The Gershwin musical is now an American classic.

THE CRADLE WILL ROCK

Book, lyrics, and music by Mark Blitzstein
Starring Howard da Silva, Will Greer, and Olive Stanton

Most musicals of the 1930's offered theatergoers escape from the blue notes of economic depression. However, the reality of the streets outside the theaters was not easy to ignore. Theatrical revues such as *New Americana* and *As Thousands Cheer* dealt with those economic and political conditions which tore at America and the world. So did the musical *The Cradle Will Rock*. The opening of this musical proved to be one of the strangest in Broadway's history.

Book: *Mr. Mister runs everything in Steeltown, all to the financial benefit of himself, his family, and a few cronies. The town's workers earn just enough from their hard labor to scrape by—but nothing more. Led by Larry Foreman, the workers at the steel plant organize to win union recognition in order to deal with Mr. Mister.*

"Junior's Gonna Go to Honolulu"
"The Nickel Under the Foot"
"Croon Spoon"

Ballads, blues, torch songs, parodies, and patter songs all gave musical variety to the production. Blitzstein's songs fit the story and drew personality pictures of the characters. However, these were the 1930's. Industrialists and financiers feared that unions might rip management control from their hands. Their representatives in Washington saw communists lurking behind the placards of worker demonstrations. They feared something similar in Blitzstein's musical.

Initial support for the production had been provided by the Federal Theater Project, which subsidized theatrical groups hurt by the Depression. As government bureaucrats grew timid about Blitzstein's story plot, they withdrew their support. Orson Welles's Mercury Theater production took over the backing, but the night the show was to open, a temporary injunction from Washington closed the theater even as the audience was arriving. Welles quickly hired an empty auditorium twenty blocks away, then led both cast and audience up the streets of Manhattan to the substitute theater. The musicians, obeying the injunction, refused to join the procession. To avoid the no-work order, the cast bought tickets and performed from their seats in the audience. Without musicians, Blitzstein played the score on the piano and described the story as he went along.

"The most versatile triumph of the politically insurgent theater."
—Brooks Atkinson,
The New York Times

Private backing carried on, allowing the show to move to a regular Broadway theater to run for four months. *The Cradle Will Rock* was revived in later years, including concert presentations of its music. In 1985, critics applauded its restaging in London's famous Old Vic Theater.

The Wizard of OZ

Lyrics by E. Y. Harburg
Music by Harold Arlen
Starring Judy Garland, Bert Lahr, Ray Bolger, Jack Haley,
and Frank Morgan

The Wizard of Oz is a movie musical based on a book by Frank L. Baum and now frequently seen on TV. However, a small television screen can't convey the visual excitement of this film as a movie theater can. This was a big production. Although Victor Fleming received credit as its director, three others worked on the film. The screenplay, that is, the book, went through numerous rewrites. Sixty-eight sets were created for the filming and 9,200 actors in all performed, including 150 midgets who took the parts of the Munchkins.

"Somewhere Over the Rainbow"

"Follow the Yellow Brick Road"

"We're Off to See the Wizard"

For all those grand statistics, memories of the show often boil down to one thing—Judy Garland singing "Somewhere Over the Rainbow." The song will always be identified with this legendary entertainer. Surprisingly, it was almost cut from the film.

Perhaps just as surprisingly, Judy Garland was not the first choice to play the part of Dorothy. The studio had first tried to get the very popular child star Shirley Temple to play the role.

Garland was not the only substitution. Jack Haley got the role of the tin man after the original choice, Buddy Ebsen, fell ill with aluminum poisoning. A tin man with metal poisoning? It could only happen in Oz.

Screenplay: *Dorothy and her dog Toto live in Kansas. When a cyclone one day whips across the flat Kansas plain, the two are caught up in it and tossed away into the land of Oz, an enchanted place of witches, tiny Munchkin people, and flying monkeys. For all its colorful wonders, Dorothy wants to return to Kansas. The Munchkins and the Good Witch of the North advise her to seek help from the wizard who rules Oz in his palace in the Emerald City. Dorothy is joined by three others: a scarecrow longing for brains, a tin man desiring a heart, and a lion seeking courage. Together they set off, singing "We're Off to See the Wizard." Before granting their wishes, the wizard orders them to get rid of the Wicked Witch of the West. After beating back attacks from the witch's forces, including flying monkeys, Dorothy manages to destroy her. Unfortunately, it turns out that the wizard is a humbug and only grants wishes by convincing people to look inside themselves for satisfaction. That is enough for her three friends, but not for Dorothy. Only with magic help from the Good Witch of the North does she finally reach Kansas.*

Book by John O'Hara
Lyrics by Lorenz Hart
Music by Richard Rodgers
Starring Gene Kelly, June Havoc, and Vivienne Segel

"Bewitched, Bothered and Bewildered"

"I Could Write a Book"

"Zip"

"Take Him"

Puts "three-dimensional" human beings on the stage was Wolcott Gibbs's praise in *The New Yorker*.

Book: *The setting is Chicago's South Side and the pal of the title is nightclub dancer Joey Evans, a hard, ambitious person willing to use anyone, but especially women, to claw his way upward. Innocent Linda English falls for Joey and helps him until he abandons her for older, more experienced Vera Simpson, who is "Bewitched, Bothered and Bewildered" by the dancer. As proof, Vera rents Joey an apartment and finances his own nightclub, which he opens as the Chez Joey. Linda tells Vera that Joey plans to blackmail her by informing her husband of the affair. Only then does Vera realize Joey has no feelings and is only using her to satisfy his ambitions. She confronts the "heel" by asking him if he could still survive if she moved to California or dropped dead. "Would you eat?"*

"I always eat," replies Joey.

"Well," says Vera, "I think I'm going to be called away to California or maybe drop dead." Catching the sarcasm, Joey knows they are finished. He walks off into the Chicago night, meets a new girl and, with his usual charm, casts his line and hooks her.

John O'Hara based his book for *Pal Joey* on stories he had written in the form of letters for *The New Yorker* magazine. With a scoundrel for a hero, a tough night club atmosphere, and a cheating wife, the show did not appeal to critics. Still, *Pal Joey* did last for 374 performances despite mixed reviews. In a more cynical period a decade later, *Pal Joey* was revived in triumph.

The decade of the 1940's had already begun when *Pal Joey* opened on December 25, 1940, and the guns of war were already booming in Europe and Asia. The United States was still at peace, however, so musicals in 1940 seemed more related to the previous decade. But those booming guns were sounding the overture for the big and tragic show about to begin: World War II.

Questions and Activities

Examining musicals

1. Discuss ways in which the production of a movie musical differs from the staging of a theater musical.

2. Three of the musicals in this chapter may be considered solely entertainment. The other three deal with real social or

political problems. Decide which three are the former and which three the latter.

3. Debate whether a musical should have a serious message or if it should exist only to entertain.

4. Can you think why Blitzstein chose the title *The Cradle Will Rock* for his protest musical?

5. Why was the song "I Got Plenty o' Nuttin'" chosen as the title song for this chapter of the 1930's?

Listening to music

1. Listen to a recording of *Porgy and Bess*. Decide what is operatic about *Porgy and Bess* and what is more like a musical.

2. *Porgy and Bess*'s "I Got Plenty o' Nuttin'" and "It Ain't Necessarily So" became pop standards. Listen to them and decide why they are still heard.

3. Cole Porter's songs are especially known for their lyrics. Find examples such as "Just One of Those Things," "Let's Do It," "Begin the Beguine," and songs from *Anything Goes* in this chapter and *Kiss Me Kate* in the next. Then enjoy the lyrics.

4. If you can see the movie *The Wizard of Oz*, consider how the color and movement of a song's film sequence match the song's spirit.

Creating a musical

Act I, Scene *iii*:

The star of our history musical has been invited to Hollywood to sing and dance in a 1930's movie musical.

1. Write the the story of what then happens in Hollywood.

2. What songs from the 1930's will our star sing?

3. Design props and costumes for this scene.

Reading the critics

1. Explain London's 17-year wait for *Porgy and Bess*, which was commented upon in that city's *Daily Herald*.

2. What did Brooks Atkinson of *The New York Times* mean with his statement about *The Cradle Will Rock*?

CHAPTER 11

The 1940's

Life changed dramatically with the outbreak of World War II. Not since the Civil War had the United States been so completely at war, and never since its end in 1945 has war touched so many American lives. This was a worldwide catastrophe. With so many men and women in the military, with gas rationing permitting only the most essential travel, and with industry working overtime, national entertainment suffered.

Still, New York boomed. When troops got ready to board ships in New York and New Jersey ports, they found time for a last fling in Manhattan before embarking for the war in Africa and Europe. Broadway marquees glowed with names of stars and shows to entertain them all.

Musical revues provided much of that entertainment. *This Is the Army* featured songs by Irving Berlin, most from World War I, with the singing cast, including Berlin, dressed in World War I uniforms. Revues such as *Sons O' Fun, Stars on Ice, Star and Garter*, and the *Ziegfeld Follies of 1943* all broke the 500 performance mark.

> "This Is the Army, Mr. Jones"
>
> "American Eagle"
>
> "Oh How I Hate to Get Up in the Morning"
>
> (songs from *This Is the Army*)

Servicemen on the town enjoyed such revues. And they enjoyed New York's Coney Island amusement park, the city's nightclubs, the lights of Times Square, and the quiet of Central Park. At least, the three sailors in the following musical enjoyed their 24 hours on the town.

ON THE TOWN

Book and lyrics by Betty Comden and Adolph Green
Music by Leonard Bernstein
Starring Sono Osato, Nancy Walker, Comden and Green

> "New York, New York"

Book: *On a 24-hour leave in New York, three sailors set out to see the sights. Gabby falls in love with Miss Turnstiles, a contest*

73

winner he sees pictured on a subway poster. Persuading his two friends to join him in search of the girl, they sing and dance in Times Square, Central Park, Coney Island, and even the Museum of Natural History.

Opening on December 28, 1944, *On The Town* was Leonard Bernstein's first broadway show. It also began the Comden-Green partnership, which would, over the years, produce many more Broadway shows. They also played two of the roles. The book idea came from dancer and choreographer Jerome Robbins, another artist whose name would frequently light up Broadway marquees in the coming decades. *On The Town* stayed in town for 463 performances and is remembered today mainly as an early collaboration of these talented personalities.

Book and lyrics by Oscar Hammerstein II
Music by Richard Rodgers
Starring Alfred Drake, Joan Roberts, Celeste Holm, Bambi Linn, and Howard da Silva

Two other names had been around Broadway for some years, but never together. When his partner Lorenz Hart grew ill (he died in 1943), composer Richard Rodgers sought a new lyricist. He found him in Oscar Hammerstein II, already well known for his work on *Show Boat* and other successful musicals. Joining forces in 1943, they produced *Oklahoma!*. Hammerstein adapted it from a 1931 play by Lynn Riggs called *Green Grow the Lilacs*. By keeping the book plot close to the story of the play, Hammerstein gave substance to the musical. He made the characters believable as actual persons, from the lonely drifter Jud to the scatterbrained flirt Ado Annie.

Choreographer Agnes de Mille had already pioneered the arrangement of ballet to American folk themes and music, a perfect approach for the dance sequences in *Oklahoma!* because of the story's rural setting. Nor were her dances simply tossed into the recipe like sugar. Instead, they nourished the story, moving the plot along with dance movements instead of words. Laurey's dream ballet expresses her fears just as Will's high-stepping routines express his Western swagger.

Like de Mille's choreography, the songs helped establish atmosphere and portray the personalities of the characters. Rodgers' opening melody lets you know that it really is a beautiful morning. The rhythm he created for "The Surrey With the Fringe on Top" jogs along like a horse's clippity-clop. Annie's admission that she "Cain't Say No," is apologetic and wistful, yet betrays a slight twinkle. The chorus number "Oklahoma" begins with a prolonged "O," then snaps into the rest of the word, shouting the pride of the people for their new state. In short, Richard Rodgers' songs are expressions of the atmosphere, feelings, and personality of the book.

Book: *The setting is the state of Oklahoma at the beginning of the twentieth century. "Oh What a Beautiful Morning!" sings Curly as he arrives at Laurey's family farm. Curly suggests taking Laurey to an upcoming box social in "The Surrey with the Fringe on Top." Will Parker turns up, having just returned from "Kansas City," where he won fifty dollars in a steer-roping contest, enough to let him marry Ado Annie. Unfortunately, Annie, who admits "I Cain't Say No" to any handsome fellow, has promised herself to a traveling Persian peddler named Ali Hakim. Curly discovers he also has a rival, gruff, burly farmhand Jud Fry. To make Curly jealous, Laurey accepts Jud's invitation to the box social. In a dream ballet, Laurey sees Jud beating up Curly before carrying her away.*

At the social Curly and Jud bid against one another for Laurey's box luncheon and the privilege of sharing it with her. Curly manages to outbid Jud and the angry farmhand storms off. In the meantime, Ado and Will agree to marry, much to the relief of the peddler. Laurey and Curly also decide to marry. As everyone prepares for the double wedding, they sing a rousing praise of their territory, which is about to become the state of "Oklahoma!" But Jud has returned to break up the wedding festivities. He challenges Curly and is killed in the ensuing fight. The local judge agrees it was self-defense, and in a snappy trial acquits Curly so that he and Laurey, now married, can ride off in a fringe-topped surrey into another beautiful day.

Book and lyrics by Oscar Hammerstein II
Music by Richard Rodgers
Starring John Raitt and Jan Clayton

Two years after *Oklahoma!* Rodgers and Hammerstein followed with *Carousel*, which some critics feel is their best work. When *Carousel* opened at the Majestic Theater, *Oklahoma!* was still playing at the St. James across the street. Rodgers and Hammerstein found themselves in competition with...themselves. Again the setting is rural America of the past, this time a Maine fishing village. Once more the themes—love and death—are both heartwarming and profound. Again Agnes de Mille demonstrated how dance could be as much a part of the story as either dialogue or song.

Book: *At a carnival, the town's inhabitants dance "The Carousel Waltz." Billy Bigelow, operator of the carnival carousel, spots Julie Jordon. Neighbors warn Julie not to become involved with this carnival barker, a drifter. Nevertheless, by the time that "June Is Bustin' Out All Over," she and Billy have married. Having left the carnival, Billy has no job, a situation made more critical when*

Julie becomes pregnant. In a **soliloquy***, (sa-ʼlil-a-kwee) a stage device in which an actor speaks his thoughts aloud, Billy ponders his prospects as an unemployed father. Financial worries force Billy to join his rowdy friend Jigger in a robbery attempt. To avoid capture, Billy kills himself. Julie grieves as her friend Nellie comforts her with the thought that "You'll Never Walk Alone."*

Years pass and Billy is allowed to return to earth to aid his growing daughter. When she refuses his gift of a star, Billy slaps her, but his love for her makes it seem like a kiss. At her school graduation, Billy's spirit sings "You'll Never Walk Alone," the unheard song giving the young girl hope and strength to face the future.

Until Hammerstein's death in 1960, virtually every musical he and Rodgers created met with success. Sometimes criticized for its sentimentality, their work appealed to mainstream America. For the millions who never visited New York and who knew their shows only from recordings and film adaptations, Rodgers and Hammerstein became synonymous with Broadway and musical theater. Some of their other works include: *South Pacific* (1949), *Flower Drum Song* (1958), *The King and I* (1951), *The Sound of Music* (1959).

Book by E. Y. Harburg and Fred Saidy
Lyrics by E. Y. Harburg
Music by Burton Lane
Starring Ella Logan, Donald Richards, and David Wayne

You have already met E. Y. Harburg as lyricist for *The Wizard of Oz*. In the 1930's he had written for revues that frequently dealt with problems of workers. His song (written to the music of Jay Gorney) "Brother, Can You Spare a Dime?" had been the theme song of the Depression years. Harburg's sympathy with labor problems inspired *Finian's Rainbow*. It was satire wrapped in fantasy, a package that most people could take.

Book: *With a crock of gold stolen from the leprechauns, Finian McLonergan and his daughter Sharon have fled to Rainbow Valley, Missitucky, U.S.A., leaving behind their beloved Glocca Morra, Ireland. Finian believes that if he plants his stolen treasure near the American gold reserves at Fort Knox, his fortune will increase. In Missitucky father and daughter stumble into a conflict between sharecroppers and the political tricks of racist Senator Billboard Rawkins. Sharon falls in love with Woody Mahoney, the sharecropper leader. In the meantime a leprechaun named Og is hot on the trail of Sharon and Finian. When Og falls in love with Sharon, he discovers it causes him to slowly become a human. Sharon uses the power of the leprechauns' crock to turn racist Rawkins black. Og uses his waning powers to make him white again. The experience, however, causes the senator to become a sympathetic, likable* *person. Og also works wonders with Susan Mahoney. Unable to speak, she expresses herself in dance. Failing with Sharon, Og gives Susan the power to talk, then promptly admits, "When I'm Not Near the Girl I Love," he will love whichever girl he is near. Sharon finds she is unable to return Woody's affection and the fantasy is broken. There is no crock of gold. There is no Glocca Morra. Perhaps there is no rainbow. Yet we all wish that we might meet some fine day in Glocca Morra.*

Kiss Me Kate

Book by Bella and Samuel Spewack
Lyrics and music by Cole Porter
Starring Alfred Drake, Patricia Morison, and Lisa Kirk

Cole Porter was one of the creative giants of American musicals. his "Begin the Beguine" and "Night and Day" live as pop classics. His hand also lay upon the songs of *Anything Goes*, a musical described in the previous chapter. There were many more Porter musicals, but *Kiss Me Kate* ranks as one of his best. Great songs fit the plot like a fashionable glove so that the story could be outlined with the songs as they neatly fall into place. That story is based upon and uses parts of Shakespeare's play *The Taming of the Shrew*. Porter even turned Shakespearean phrases into song.

Book: *Opening night for a musical production of* The Taming of the Shrew *looms but hours away. The two stars, Lilli Vanessi and Fred Graham, recently divorced, speak with one another only when quarreling. Two other romantically tied performers, Lois Land and Bill Calhoun, also have problems. Such nervous tension seems aggravated by "Another Op'nin', Another Show." In Lilli's dressing room the star tells Fred that she has become engaged to wealthy Harrison Howell. Still, they fondly remember their first show together when they danced and sang "Wunderbar." Two gangsters interrupt to collect on a gambling IOU that Bill has forged with Fred's name. When Fred claims not to remember it, the gunmen give him time but promise to return. Receiving a bouquet of flowers from Fred, Lilli admits she is still "So in Love" with her ex-husband. Tucking the bouquet card in her costume without reading it, she fails to realize Fred had meant the flowers for Lois.*

The Taming of the Shrew *performance begins. In Shakespeare's plot Katherina, played by Lilli, and Petruchio, played by Fred, square off against one another. As Kate (Lilli) begins an argument with Petruchio (Fred), she pulls the flower card from her costume to discover that the bouquet had been meant for Lois. The scene ends in an actual slugging match between Lilli and Fred.*

During the intermission, angry Lilli decides to leave the show. Just then the gangsters arrive to collect on the IOU. Fred cannot pay if Lilli walks out and the play closes. Therefore, the gunmen force Lilli to remain. Harrison Howell shows up to claim Lilli and meets

Lois, who realizes she once had a brief fling with Howell. She reassures Bill that "I'm Always True to You in My Fashion," even if that fashion might be somewhat suspect. When Harrison describes how easy and comfortable life will be with him, Lilli decides better Fred than boredom and returns to her ex-husband. The gangsters learn their boss has been "rubbed out," so the IOU no longer means anything.

Fred and Lilli go back onstage to conclude The Taming of the Shrew, *which ends as Petruchio (Fred) embraces Kate (Lilli) with "Kiss Me Kate."*

The decade of the 1940's was a watershed in American and world history. It began with one of history's most terrible wars. It ended with the Cold War, which would last almost a half century. Perhaps because of the seriousness of the period, the American musical had matured. Going beyond mere entertainment, musicals began to be built around serious themes, deal with down-to-earth problems, and picture realistic personalities, even if one of them was a leprechaun inclined to fall in love.

Kiss Me Kate

Questions and Activities

Examining musicals

1. What places would a musical story visit if its characters were shown "on the town" in your town or region?

2. The granting of statehood was the climactic event in *Oklahoma!*. Think of an event in the history of your town or state that could be adapted for a musical.

3. Of the Shakespeare plays you know, which would you choose to adapt as a musical?

4. Explain how you would adapt the play mentioned in the exercise above.

Listening to music

1. Locate some recordings of the major Rodgers and Hammerstein musicals.

   a. Of the listed song titles, which are you already familiar with?

   b. Listen to the songs and select your favorites.

   c. Discuss how each song fits into the story.

2. *Oklahoma!* and *Carousel* have been filmed. If you can see videos of the movies, describe how the dance numbers fit into the story plot.

3. Rodgers and Hammerstein usually included at least one uplifting and inspiring song in each of their musicals. Pick one from a work you hear and discuss its message.

Creating a musical

Act I, Scene *iv*:

This World War II portion of our history musical takes the star to war-torn Europe and the Pacific to entertain the troops.

1. Include war events in the story of this scene.

2. What songs will the star sing on this tour?

3. Design wartime costumes and scenery for this scene.

Reading the critics

1. What did Brooks Atkinson of *The New York Times* mean by "the highest judge" and "the ultimate verdict" when writing about *Carousel*, and why did such lofty praise fit this musical?

2. Do you agree with Otis Guernsey that *Carousel* demonstrated how music and real drama could be good entertainment? Why do you think he referred to opera in making this judgment?

CHAPTER 12

The 1950's

The artistic life of Europe went into hibernation during World War II. Many of the Continent's theatrical artists had fled the dismal philosophy of fascism (ˈfash-izm) and then the devastation of war; a number of them ended up in Hollywood or on Broadway. With the cultural centers of Europe forced to rebuild after their spiritual and material destruction, only one artistic capital flourished following the war: New York City.

The city was also the world's financial capital. As Wall Street prospered, Broadway flourished, with the financiers willingly backing musicals, making productions ever more lavish. The 1950's enjoyed some of the most memorable musicals. The decade also saw the usual forgettable flops. Producing a Broadway musical will always be a high-stakes gamble. So let us begin with gamblers.

Book by Jo Swerling and Abe Burrows
Lyrics and music by Frank Loesser
Starring Robert Alda, Vivian Blaine, Sam Levene, and
   Isabel Bigley

"…(best of 1950 due to its) originality and its avoidance of the usual musical comedy patterns."

—John Chapman,
   New York Daily News

The stories of Damon Runyon tell of star-struck actors and actresses, con men, bookies, gamblers, and tough-talking mobsters. Runyon created a way of speaking for his characters that was more "New York" than that of real New Yorkers, so it was termed Runyonesque. Runyonesque also were such characters as Nathan Detroit, Sky Masterson, Harry the Horse, Angie the Ox, and Nicely Nicely Johnson. If you haven't read about them in Runyon's stories, then meet them in *Guys and Dolls*, a "fable of Broadway."

The story for the book of *Guys and Dolls* was based on Runyon's "The Idyll of Miss Sarah Brown," but several of the musical's characters were borrowed from other Runyon stories. The idea of putting Runyon on the musical stage had been conceived of before the book for *Guys and Dolls* was written. Working with the idea, ten different writers had tried for an adaptation, but the producers rejected all their efforts. Only when radio script writer Abe Burrows took the book in hand did Harry the Horse, Sky Masterson, Miss Adelaide, and Sarah Brown prepare to sing.

Book: *When the curtains part on* Guys and Dolls, *the imagination has no farther to travel than the streets outside the theater, where hustlers and pickpockets mingle with tourists and tinhorns. Tinhorns? These typical Times Square types discuss the day's race-track picks in "A Fugue for Tinhorns." Through the midtown color marches a Salvation Army band led by beautiful but righteous Sister Sarah Brown. Into the mix saunters Nathan Detroit, hoping to find somewhere to hold one of his notorious crap games, "The Oldest Established Permanent Floating Crap Game in New York." It will not be easy because a police order has made such illegal enterprises difficult to arrange.*

"A Bushel and a Peck"
"If I Were a Bell"
"Luck Be a Lady Tonight!"
"Take Back Your Mink"

Enter Sky Masterson, a handsome high roller. Sky kids Nathan about his problems with his girlfriend Miss Adelaide, betting that he, Sky, can win any girl he goes after. Nathan takes the bet for one thousand dollars, challenging Sky to successfully invite Sister Sarah to an evening in Havana.

When the Salvation Army general threatens to close Sister Sarah's mission because of low attendance, Sky offers to provide her with a dozen genuine sinners, if she will accept his invitation for dinner—in Havana. When Nathan notices Sarah is not marching with the army band, he knows he has lost his thousand-dollar bet.

Back from Havana at four a.m. in New York, both Sister Sarah and Sky admit "I've Never Been In Love Before." Her feelings quickly cool when a police raid chases Nathan's crap game out of the mission building. Despite her change of heart, Sky promises to provide the mission with a dozen sinners. Shooting craps and pleading "Luck Be a Lady Tonight!" he compels the losers to attend a mission service. Sarah meets Adelaide; both agree they should "Marry the Man Today" and stop trying to reform them. Sky dons a mission uniform, and Nathan knows he and Adelaide will be next at the altar.

Book by Betty Comden and Adolph Green
Songs by Arthur Freed and Nacio Herb Brown
Starring Gene Kelly, Donald O'Connor, and Debbie Reynolds

SINGIN' IN THE RAIN

Fred Astaire left Broadway for Hollywood in the 1930's. Gene Kelly did the same in the 1940's. A star of many musicals, he

"You Were Meant for Me"

"The Wedding of the Painted Doll"

"Singin' in the Rain"

"One of the best musicals of the century.... In taste, intelligence, skill and delight *My Fair Lady* is the finest musical in years."

—Brooks Atkinson,
The New York Times

danced in Academy Award-winning *An American in Paris* in 1951, earning a special honor for his contribution to the art of movie choreography. A year later later he choreographed, co-directed, and starred in *Singin' in the Rain*.

Screenplay: *At a 1927 movie premiere, a reporter interviews stars Don Lockwood and Lina Lamont. Lamont, caught in the trap of many silent movie stars facing the changeover to sound, avoids public exposure of her raspy, irritating voice, so Don does most of the talking, describing his rise to stardom in films. A diction coach has been hired to help solve Lina's voice problem and save Don's newest movie. When Lina attempts songs such as "Moses Supposes," the diction coach moans. Throughout the filming, Lina and Don quarrel bitterly. While the two stars bicker, Don's romance with chorus girl Kathy Selby thrives, carrying the story's main romantic interest.*

The theme of *Singin' in the Rain* is Hollywood itself; the film makes fun of movie making in the first days of sound. Its songs are borrowed from early movie musicals. For example, "The Wedding of the Painted Doll" and "You Were Meant for Me" were first heard in *The Broadway Melody* in 1929.

The title song came from another movie of the same year (1929) entitled *Hollywood Revue*. However, movie fans will always think of "Singin' in the Rain" as Gene Kelly sang and danced it in the 1952 movie. Nonchalant yet upbeat, debonair yet cocky, Kelly danced along a street in a downpour, skipping, strutting, stepping over puddles, swinging around a light pole, striding, and singing in the drenching rain.

Book and lyrics by Alan Jay Lerner
Music by Frederick Loewe
Starring Rex Harrison, Julie Andrews, and Stanley Holloway

Playwright George Bernard Shaw wrote *Pygmalion* in 1912. He based his story idea on the Greek myth in which a sculptor named Pygmalion falls in love with a statue he has carved. After the play's success a number of producers sought permission to turn it into a musical. Shaw turned them all down. He did, however, permit movie producer Gabriel Pascal to make a film of the play. Shaw even wrote an additional scene for the movie in which Eliza attends a society ball. The scene would be included in the musical.

After Shaw died in 1950, Pascal obtained the rights to the play itself and and began looking for someone to turn it into a musical. He first approached Rodgers and Hammerstein, who rejected the project. So did Cole Porter, Leonard Bernstein, Betty

Prof. Henry Higgins

Why Can't The

English

?

"Wouldn't It Be Loverly?"

"With a Little Bit of Luck"

"I Could Have Danced All Night"

"I've Grown Accustomed to Her Face"

The Rain In Spain

Hurricanes hardly

happen

Comden and Adolph Green, as well as opera composer Gian-Carlo Menotti. He then asked Alan Jay Lerner and Frederick Loewe, who had collaborated on *Brigadoon* and *Paint Your Wagon*. They accepted, but then Pascal died and project plans came to a halt. Nevertheless, Lerner and Loewe had become too interested to forget the adaptation idea, so they acquired the rights for *Pygmalion* from the Shaw estate and set to work on *My Fair Lady*.

An unusual feature of the production of *My Fair Lady* was its financial backing. With the introduction of 33⅓ rpm, long-playing records, recordings of Broadway musicals had become very popular. Realizing this, Columbia Records put up the complete cost of $400,000 to produce the musical in order to obtain the rights to record the original cast production. Columbia easily earned that back, as *My Fair Lady* became the most profitable musical, and the recording the best-selling musical show album, up to that time. After years of negotiating, Shaw's play had blossomed into the musical story of a poor London flower girl who became *My Fair Lady*.

Book: *Outside London's opera house in Covent Garden, Professor Henry Higgins, linguistic expert, takes notes of neighborhood speech habits while lamenting to Colonel Pickering, another linguist, "Why Can't the English?" learn to speak properly. Noting the dialect of flower seller Eliza Doolittle, who displays her London cockney speech with sentences such as "Wouldn't It Be Loverly?," he claims he can better a person's station in life by improving his or her speech.*

Overhearing the boast, Eliza shows up at the professor's home anxious to take him up on it. The comic give-and-take as Higgins, a self-centered man certain of his abilities, bullies Eliza carries the story to the climactic moment when Eliza manages to repeat "The Rain in Spain" and other tongue twisters properly.

Higgins then escorts Eliza to the races at Ascot and to a fashionable ball. Despite some humorous mistakes, Eliza, through speech and manner, passes herself off as a lady, and not just as a lady, but as a princess. Congratulating himself on her success, Higgins (and Pickering) forget that it was Eliza's perseverance that made the experiment succeed.

Feeling ignored and hurt, Eliza leaves Higgins's home for that of his mother, the one person who has offered her sympathy throughout. Higgins, to his surprise, discovers that "I've Grown Accustomed to Her Face" and actually misses Eliza. Listening to recordings of her voice in his home, he muses on the fact Eliza has left. She quietly returns as the curtain descends.

Book by Arthur Laurents
Lyrics by Stephen Sondheim
Music by Leonard Bernstein
Starring Carol Lawrence, Larry Kert, and Chita Rivera

Guys and Dolls pictures the shadier side of New York life in a spirit of fun and satire. It is a comedy. *West Side Story* also deals with New York's bleaker environment. But it is a tragedy, an unhappy picture of life on slum streets, of youth gangs pitted against one another with hate and death. Despite the theme, *West Side Story* was a musical triumph. Still, its negative portrayal of life in New York kept the U.S. government from allowing it to be shown at the Brussels World's Fair or to tour the Soviet Union.

The idea of fitting the theme of Shakespeare's *Romeo and Juliet* to a modern musical had come to choreographer and director Jerome Robbins in 1949. Cole Porter's 1948 take-off on Shakespeare, *Kiss Me Kate,* may have inspired him. If you are familiar with *Romeo and Juliet,* you know that this most famous of love stories tells of two young lovers kept apart by their feuding families. When the two tragically die, the families at last realize the senselessness of their anger and the feud ends.

The first book idea was to set the musical on New York's East Side, where a Jewish girl and Catholic boy would fall in love amid the displeasure of their families. Because this resembled a popular radio program plot, the concept was changed to two street gangs serving as the feuding families and the site moved to Manhattan's West Side. One gang, the Jets, considers itself "American" and is led by Riff. Bernardo leads a Puerto Rican gang called the Sharks. When Tony, an old member of the Jets, falls in love with Bernardo's sister Maria, the Romeo-Juliet theme falls into place.

Book: *Riff plans to challenge Bernardo and the Sharks to a fight at the gym dance. However, the central encounter at the gym is Tony dancing with Maria and falling in love. As they later sit on the fire escape of Maria's apartment building, recalling the famous balcony scene in* Romeo and Juliet, *Maria and Tony admit that "Tonight" was not just an ordinary night but something special.*

At a neighborhood drugstore the Jets and Sharks challenge one another to a rumble. Tony intercedes and urges the two leaders to fight without weapons the following night. When the gangs do meet beneath the columns of an overhead highway, Tony again appears to try to make peace. Bernardo, angry that Tony has been seeing his sister, pushes him. Riff jumps into the fray. He is knifed. Tony knifes Bernardo and the Sharks' leader dies.

"The dance is fully as important here as the spoken word in carrying the taut story line."
—*Theater Arts*

"...the bitter story unfolds as a 'catastrophic roar.'"
—Walter Kerr,
New York Herald Tribune

"Jet Song"
"Maria"
"Tonight"
"I Feel Pretty"
"Somewhere"

The second act opens as Maria prepares to meet Tony. One of the Sharks tells her that Tony has killed her brother, and then races off to gun down Tony. Tony appears on Maria's fire escape balcony where the two sing that "Somewhere" there must be a place free from hate and fighting. The song merges into an emotional ballet, after which Tony departs. Falling for a story meant to trap him, Tony is told that Maria has been killed. The ruse works and Tony is shot by one of the Sharks. The story ends as the two gangs, frightened and sick of more deaths, join to carry off Tony's body.

West Side Story demonstrated that a musical can handle a serious theme, can be a tragedy and make people think, and can also entertain them. Jerome Robbins's choreography and direction made it a great stage spectacle. Leonard Bernstein's score made it a great musical experience. Altogether, *West Side Story* was an excellent theatrical work.

Book, music, and lyrics by Meredith Willson Starring Robert Preston and Barbara Cook

While the book of *West Side Story* is serious and heavy, that of *The Music Man* is light and entertaining. In fact, it hardly has a story at all. Yet on that story hangs a delightful comedy with marvelous music of great variety, proving again that it is music above all that makes a musical succeed. The songs of *The Music Man* are catchy, singable, of entertaining variety, and well worked into the entire production. Perhaps such theatrical coordination resulted because book, lyrics, and score were all the creation of one person.

Meredith Willson had grown up in a small Iowa town in the early years of the twentieth century, the place and time in which *The Music Man* is set. After music study in New York, Willson became a radio orchestra leader. His native talent and folksy

86

"Marian the Librarian"

"Trouble"

"Goodnight My Someone"

"Seventy-six Trombones"

"Till There Was You"

humor combined to make *The Music Man* a rousing success. On its opening night the audience began clapping rhythmically in time to the snappy music. The show business paper *Variety* wrote, "Nothing like it [the audience response] has ever been seen on Broadway."

Book: *Harold Hill comes to River City, Iowa, by train to pull off his usual swindle. The scheme is to sell the townspeople on the idea of buying band instruments and uniforms for their children, whom Hill will then teach to play music. However, before the instruments and uniforms arrive, Hill plans to disappear.*

Love upsets Hill's scheme when he falls for "Marian the Librarian." When she discovers Hill's plans, she threatens to expose him, forcing him to stay on in River City until the instruments actually arrive. Once they do come, Hill is obliged to teach the town youngsters to play them, although he knows nothing about music himself.

Hill does the best he can, training the youthful orchestra for a public performance, although certain he will be run out of town when parents hear their children play. Come the concert, the band blasts out a loud, discordant blare.

To Hill's surprise the town's parents, proud of their children, think the din is beautiful and Hill's reputation is saved.

The part of Harold Hill had been offered to comedian Danny Kaye, dancers Gene Kelly and Dan Dailey, and band leader Phil Harris. All turned down the role. It was taken by veteran movie actor Robert Preston and became the most important role of his career. He sang rapid patter songs, explaining his sales technique to the clackity-clack rhythm of a train and prophesying with an evangelist's passion the trouble that idleness would cause River City's children if they didn't learn music. The show's most popular song, "Seventy-six Trombones," excited not only the residents of River City but the theater audience as well. *The Music Man* told the story of a music salesman who did not know music. It told the story with great music and that is why it is a memorable musical.

The 1950's enjoyed other long-running musicals, with *The King and I, The Sound of Music, Pajama Game,* and *Damn Yankees* all running for more than 1,000 performances. Original cast recordings became best-selling albums. Most importantly, musicals of the 1950's embraced a great variety of themes, musical styles, and staging concepts. The American musical had certainly come of age.

Questions and Activities

Examining musicals

1. The heroes of *Guys and Dolls* are gamblers and scoundrels. The hero of *The Music Man* is a swindler. Why do such characters appeal to audiences?

2. Considering the Cold War situation of the 1950's, do you think it was proper for the U.S. government to refuse to send *West Side Story* on foreign tours?

3. Why do you suppose "The Oldest Established..." was chosen as the chapter's title song?

4. What reasons might Shaw have had for refusing to let his play *Pygmalion* be turned into a musical?

Listening to music

1. Listen to dance music from *West Side Story*—"Jet Song" or "Dance at the Gym," for example. Would any of it make suitable music for a dance at your school?

2. Chapter 6 told how natural physical movements, amplified with music, become dance. If you can see the movie of *West Side Story*, pick out the natural movements used for dance steps.

3. Listen to such patter songs as "I'm an Ordinary Man" or "A Hymn to Him" from *My Fair Lady,* or "Trouble" from *The Music Man.* Copy some of the lyrics, then read them aloud to catch their underlying rhythm.

4. The settings and spirits of the musicals in this chapter differ greatly. Listen to recordings of these shows and discuss how their music styles support the special atmosphere of each story.

Creating a musical

Act I, Scene *v*:

The star of our history musical has become a famous performer, starring in a number of Broadway shows.

1. In which big shows from this chapter's decade will you have the star appear?

2. What songs will the star sing?

Reading the critics

1. What are examples of the "originality and avoidance of usual musical comedy patterns" that John Chapman saw in *Guys and Dolls*?

2. What might Walter Kerr have meant by "catastrophic roar" in his review of *West Side Story*?

CHAPTER 13

The 1960's

Events of the 1960's had such an impact on American emotions that they are still vividly remembered. The United States began bombing North Vietnam in 1965, and by 1969, 550,000 Americans were fighting in Southeast Asia. President John Kennedy, his brother Robert, Malcolm X, and Martin Luther King, Jr., fell to assassins. NASA brought the decade to a climax when Neil Armstrong stepped on the moon on July 20, 1969. The decade's themes were the Vietnam War, civil rights, women's liberation, and new social attitudes. Its music was rock and roll. Broadway seemed to ignore it all. Only with the invasion of the rock opera *Hair* at the decade's end would political and social concerns reach a musical stage.

As for musicals themselves, the maturing of this American art in the 1950's continued into the 1960's. The decade produced some of the most lasting musicals, and those musicals demonstrated a variety of music and book ideas.

Book by Michael Stewart
Lyrics and music by Jerry Herman
Starring Carol Channing

Basically, there was nothing out of the ordinary about *Hello, Dolly!* Like many musicals before it, it was a period piece, set in New York and its Yonkers suburb in the 1890's. That allowed for nostalgia and all the wistful staging of an innocent past that American audiences love. Its book, based on Thornton Wilder's play *The Matchmaker*, involved trapping a reluctant widower into marriage. Fluff for a book? Perhaps, but the musical had a star and a song that made it the longest-running musical up to that time.

The star was Carol Channing, who played the noisy busybody whose business card reads, "Dolly Levi—financial consultation, guitar and mandolin instruction, varicose veins reduced." As a matchmaker she confessed that her major occupation was "to meddle." Playing Dolly, Carol Channing was either a purring kitten or a rampaging tiger, slinking or ripping across the stage as the occasion demanded.

The title song was an instant hit. Within a year over 100 recordings of that song were made in the United States and Europe. Louis Armstrong recorded the most popular version, making the show a success even before anyone saw it. Everyone wanted to hear Channing sing the song as she entered the Harmonia Gardens restaurant. But they were kept waiting for the song until the second act, a real teaser of pacing. Nobody dared walk out on Dolly.

"Miss Channing is a complete delight whether she is dancing, singing in that inimitable voice or just sitting at a table eating."

—Howard Taubman,
The New York Times

Book: *As a matchmaker, Dolly plans to wed "half-a-millionaire" Horace Vandergelder herself. Timid of Dolly's powerhouse come-on, he accepts her suggestion for two other marriage prospects, hat shop owner Irene Molloy and wealthy Ernestina Money. Vandergelder leaves his clerks Barnaby and Cornelius in charge of the Yonkers store in order to meet the two candidates in Manhattan. The clerks close the store and sneak off to the city themselves. Unaware their boss is destined for Miss Molloy's shop, they head there just before Vandergelder's arrival.*

When his hopes for Miss Molloy are dashed, Vandergelder allows Dolly to arrange a rendezvous with Ernestine Money at the Harmonia Gardens Restaurant. In the meantime Dolly has reserved a table herself, hoping to attract Vandergelder "Before the Parade (of life) Passes By." To make the evening more interesting, Cornelius and Barnaby take Miss Molloy and her assistant to the same restaurant.

Dolly is well known at the Harmonia Gardens, so when she arrives the waiters and restaurant staff enthusiastically greet her with "Hello, Dolly!" The audience sits up to finally hear the great number, then settles down to see how Dolly will capture Vandergelder. Ernestine Money exits, Dolly takes over and an exasperated Vandergelder complains, "Dolly, anybody who married you..."

"Why, Horace Vandergelder, I have no intention of marrying you!" replies Dolly.

When Vandergelder discovers his daughter singing in the restaurant with her boyfriend and his two clerks eating at another table, he starts a brawl that lands everyone in court. There Dolly talks the judge into freeing them all. If the judge cannot resist Dolly's line, Vandergelder realizes he cannot either, so he gives up and agrees to marry her.

92

The part of Dolly was first offered to Ethel Merman, who turned it down, so it is Carol Channing who is most remembered as Dolly. After 1,272 performances, she was replaced by Fred Astaire's dance partner Ginger Rogers. More big names took the role during its long run, including Martha Raye, Betty Grable, Phyllis Diller, and Pearl Bailey. Then Merman finally took the role she had once refused. Barbara Streisand played the movie version of Dolly.

Although the title song dominates memories, the musical had many other fine numbers, from the march tempo "Before the Parade Passes By" through the snappy "Put On Your Sunday Clothes" to the romantic "It Only Takes a Moment."

As "Hello, Dolly!" was sweeping the country, a composer named Mack David said that its tune came from "Sunflower," a song he had written in 1948. On examination his claim appeared to be just. Dolly's composer Jerry Herman agreed to pay David $500,000 for the rights to the tune he had "borrowed," the most money ever awarded in a song copyright suit.

Had Herman stolen the 1940's song? Probably not intentionally. It was likely an unconscious borrowing. Having once heard the original years earlier, Herman must have had the tune lodged in the back of his mind, only to have it pop up as his own invention when he composed the score for *Hello, Dolly!*

Book by Joseph Stein
Lyrics by Sheldon Harnick
Music by Jerry Bock
Starring Zero Mostel, Maria Karnilova, and Beatrice Arthur

Although this musical was set at the beginning of the century and included a matchmaker, as did *Hello, Dolly!*, it was entirely different in story, sound, setting, and staging.

"Tradition"

"Matchmaker, Matchmaker"

"If I Were a Rich Man"

"Sunrise, Sunset"

"Anatevka"

Book: *As the musical opens, Tevye the milkman explains how "Tradition" supports the people of the poor Russian village of Anatevka. Symbolizing those important traditions, a man sits on the roof of one of the houses playing a fiddle. As the story progresses, Tevye sees new ideas tearing away at the traditional Jewish values he so cherishes.*

First, his oldest daughter Tzeitel refuses to marry the well-to-do butcher that the village matchmaker has chosen for her. Instead, she wishes to wed Motel the tailor, to which Tevye, because of his love for his daughter, consents. His second daughter Hodel has fallen in love with Perchik, a political radical. Although Tevye cannot see what love has to do with marriage, he also gives in to her wishes, then watches ruefully as Perchik is exiled to Siberia to be

You
Do

Love Me?

Do I

love you?

followed by Hodel, "Far From the Home I Love." When his third daughter, Chava, decides to marry a Christian, it is too much and Tevye refuses.

The blow falls heavily when Chava elopes. Nor has Tevye time to recover before the czar's constable arrives to tell the villagers that they must leave Anatevka, shattering the little bit that remains of Tevye's world. As the villagers depart, Tevye and his wife Golde bound for America, they sing of their love for "Anatevka." How can they survive in a new world? Tevye turns and beckons the fiddler down from the house roof, realizing that only by taking his traditions with him can he manage.

Joseph Stein based his book on Eastern European stories written by Russian-born Shalom Aleichem. Jerry Bock adapted traditional Jewish and Eastern European music for his score. Neither copied directly but used the sources for inspiration, translating the spirit and substance for the Broadway stage.

The book's serious plot still leaves room for humor. Tevye moans in prayer to God about his sorry lot and how much more deeply he could worship "If I Were a Rich Man." When he discovers his daughters wish to marry for love, an untraditional idea, he asks his wife Golde, "Do You Love Me?" She laughs at such a ridiculous question, feeling that her endless days of washing clothes, raising children, cooking, and working for their life together should be enough of an answer.

Much of the initial success of *Fiddler on the Roof* rode on the broad back of Zero Mostel, who played the part of Tevye. Mostel turned down the part when Stein first sent the actor-comedian the script for consideration. Character actor Walter Matthau, veteran of many movies and plays, was then asked to audition. As he was reading the part, he paused and said that the proper person for the role was Zero Mostel. A voice from the darkened auditorium replied, "If we could get Zero, do you think you'd be reading for it?"

The script was reworked and Mostel was approached once more. This time he accepted, and went on to create the part of Tevye the milkman.

The book and musical were much stronger than one man. After Mostel left the show, it ran on with others playing the lead for 3,242 performances, longer than *Hello, Dolly!* Translated into several languages, the musical became popular in central Europe, where its story and music struck familiar chords. There it is titled *Anatevka*, the little village that became a big musical.

"No smash, no blockbuster, may have a chance for a moderate success."

—*Variety* (reviewing *Fiddler on the Roof* before its New York opening)

"A cinch to satisfy almost anyone who enjoys the musical theater."

—*Variety* (reviewing *Fiddler on the Roof* after its New York opening)

94

CABARET

Book by Joe Masteroff
Lyrics by Fred Ebb
Music by John Kander
Starring Jill Haworth, Lotte Lenya, and Joel Grey

"Willkommen"
"The Money Song"
"Tomorrow Belongs to Me"
"Cabaret"

**Willkommen
bien venue
welcome**

"A marionette's-eye view of a time and a place in our lives that was brassy, wanton, carefree and doomed to crumble."

—Walter Kerr,
Herald Tribune

Christopher Isherwood had written about Germany's social decay as the Nazis rose to power in the early 1930's. John van Druten turned those stories into a play that in turn became the movie *I Am a Camera*. *Cabaret* was its musical adaptation.

Book: The musical begins as a heavily made-up master of ceremonies welcomes the audience to the Kit Kat Klub in English, French, and German, with "Willkommen." Next seen is young American writer Cliff Bradshaw approaching Berlin on a train. On board the train a German named Ernst Ludwig talks Cliff into smuggling some money through customs. Once in Berlin, Cliff finds a room at a home run by Frau Schneider, an older woman who hopes to marry Herr Schultz. Cliff falls for Sally Bowles, an English singer at the Kit Kat Klub. Dismayed by her happy-go-lucky attitude, Cliff complains that she lives in a dream when she refuses to acknowledge Berlin's political turmoil. Cliff does not, especially after he realizes the money he has been smuggling for Ernst is for the Nazi party, of which Ernst is a member. Ernst warns Frau Schneider not to marry Herr Schultz because he is a Jew, a point made dramatic when someone throws a stone through a window of her rooming house.

At the Kit Kat Klub Ernst's Nazi friends beat up Cliff as Sally sings that life is nothing more than a "Cabaret." Cliff, fed up with Berlin, the Nazis, and Sally, leaves Germany on a train as the Kit Kat Klub master of ceremonies returns to wish the audience, "adieu, good-bye, auf Wiedersehen."

In the original cast Frau Schneider was played by Lotte Lenya, widow of Kurt Weill who, with Bertolt Brecht, had written *The Threepenny Opera* in 1927 in Berlin. When the Nazis came to power Brecht, Weill, and Lenya fled Germany, ending up in the United States. Weill composed music for several Broadway musicals before his death in 1950. *The Threepenny Opera*, translated into English by Marc Blitzstein, became a long-running musical in New York's Greenwich Village. Its style and spirit influenced *Cabaret*; therefore, it was fitting that Weill's widow Lotte Lenya, who had played in the original German and English versions of *The Threepenny Opera*, should appear in *Cabaret*.

Book and lyrics by Gerome Ragni and James Rado
Music by Galt MacDermot
*With Steve Curry, Lamont Washington, Diane Keaton,
    Gerome Ragni, James Rado, and others*

The late 1960's were a time of student political activism and social rebellion. Young men protested against the Vietnam War, burnt their draft cards, and left the country. Students marched in support of civil rights. They asked for and took greater freedom with sex, drugs, and personal expression. It was a unique period in American history. Then along came *Hair*.

Whereas most musicals offer escape from the social and political tensions of a period, *Hair* set those tensions to music and sang them aloud.

Because music is used throughout, *Hair* has been described as a rock opera. Neither part of the term is exactly correct, since it is not exactly an opera nor is all the music in a rock style. Besides rock, *Hair* uses jazz, country, and the music of India, all styles that were popular in the 1960's. Its authors described *Hair* as a non-book musical, because it has very little plot, just enough of a story upon which to string its songs.

"Aquarius"

"Manchester, England"

"Good Morning Starshine"

"Let the Sunshine In"

Book: *The cast consists of a cross-section of young Americans living the pop styles of the 1960's. They are drop-outs, draft dodgers, druggies. If there is a principal character, it could be Brooklyn-born Claude, who claims he comes from Manchester, England. He shares an apartment with Berger and Sheila, a protester from N.Y.U. Claude's own girlfriend Jeannie is pregnant, but not with his child. The group is filled out with Woof, Hud, and a host of other young friends to sing about "Hashish," "Sodomy," "Air" (pollution), "Black Boys," "White Boys," and "Walking in Space." The only plot problem is whether Claude should avoid the army by burning his draft card. Rejecting the idea, Claude is called up. When his friends learn he has been killed, they gather to grieve his death as an unwarranted loss.*

Hair's power is found in the messages within its songs. The opening song, "Aquarius," sings of the dawn of a new age in which sympathy and understanding will prevail. That was a hope of the 1960's protest movements. The closing "Let the Sunshine In" sings of the same hope that opened the show. Like "Aquarius," it became a popular song.

Hair originally opened off-Broadway at the New York Shakespeare Festival Public Theater. Refusing to die at the end of its scheduled eight-week run, the play found space in a run-down dance hall, but then that building faced demolition. With extensive rewriting, producer Bertrand Castelli and director Tom O'Horgan moved this off-Broadway smash to Broadway's Biltmore on April 29, 1968.

Hair's New York runs, both off-Broadway and then longer at the Biltmore, ran to 1,844 performances. Other companies staged it around the country. It became a hit in London and Paris, where it was altered considerably to include French and English references. The same modifications occurred in every country where *Hair* was produced. The lack of a substantial book makes such changes possible, so that *Hair* can become a different show from one place to another.

Hair could only have been created in the 1960's. It was of its time. Yet, that does not do away with its musical value. It still strikes a response today, just as the events and attitudes of the 1960's are still making an impact.

Hello, Dolly!, *Fiddler on the Roof*, and *Cabaret* make no book references to the 1960's. Yet they survive as great musicals in film, summer stock, and revivals. Despite the political and social turmoil outside the theaters, the decade of the 1960's contributed significantly to the art of the American musical.

> "Hair...the frankest show in town."
>
> "The first Broadway musical in some time to have the authentic voice of today rather than the day before yesterday."
>
> "Brilliant, fresh, sheer fun."
>
> —Clive Barnes,
> *The New York Times*

Questions and Activities

Examining musicals

1. Songs are strictly protected by copyright laws.

    a. Why is this necessary?

    b. Why should Jerry Herman have been willing to pay a half million dollars for the rights to the melody of his own song, "Hello, Dolly!"?

2. What concerns of your generation could be included in a musical, just as the youthful themes of the 1960's were expressed in *Hair*?

3. Name some current pop songs that could be used in a musical based on the themes of your generation.

4. In what ways was the chapter's title song "Walking in Space" an appropriate choice?

Listening to music

1. Each show in this chapter used very different song styles, including a traditional musical style, an Eastern European style, a cabaret style, and the new sounds of rock. Listen to recordings of the music and try to hear how these styles differ.

2. Listen carefully to other songs in *Hello, Dolly!* In your opinion, could the show have been a success without the title song?

Creating a musical

Act I, Scene *vi*:

This is the final scene of the history musical's first act. Age has brought an end to our star's singing and acting career. There are no more Broadway show offers. It seems to be the star's finish.

1. Fill out the story of the star's disappointment, frustration, and depression.

2. Select songs from the shows of this chapter that would fit the musical situation.

3. Costumes and props will be those of the 1960's.

Reading the critics

1. Can you explain the differing estimates of *Fiddler on the Roof* as stated by *Variety*—the first after the reviewer saw the pre-opening tryout and the second after the Broadway opening?

2. What time and place in his readers' lives is Walter Kerr talking about in his review of *Cabaret*?

CHAPTER 14

Off-Broadway

For decades, most American musicals aimed for that small bull's-eye where Broadway angles across Times Square in midtown Manhattan. As time passed, rising production costs made it necessary that audiences fill Broadway's large theaters in order for producers to earn back the cost of staging a show. To ensure those large audiences, producers insisted upon elaborate staging and spectacular chorus numbers, which increased costs even more. This meant staging musicals in the spirit of *Hello, Dolly!*, lavish entertainments that would be sure of commercial success.

But what about composers and writers who wanted to stage musicals with less spectacular goals and had no chance to break onto Broadway? How could they realize their dreams? Knowing they could not get backing for small productions in uptown theaters, they opened in small theaters in other New York neighborhoods, notably Greenwich Village in lower Manhattan. Such off-Broadway productions were staged with minimum scenery, unknown performers, small orchestras, and as little cost as possible. Off-Broadway theaters had been attracting audiences for more than a decade when *The Fantasticks* opened at the Sullivan Street Playhouse on May 3, 1960.

Book and lyrics by Tom Jones
Music by Harvey Schmidt
Starring Jerry Orbach, Rita Gardner, and Kenneth Nelson

The show's backers invested less than $20,000 to produce *The Fantasticks*. Yet, it appeared as if they might lose even that small investment when critics turned deaf ears to its musical charms. Then word-of-mouth praise among theatergoers helped build the show's reputation. When its opening song "Try To Remember" became nationally popular, *The Fantasticks* settled

The Fantasticks

"Try to Remember"
"Soon It's Gonna Rain"
"Much More"

into its off-Broadway home to stay for decades. It still plays on Sullivan Street as this is being written in the 1990's.

Book: "Try to Remember" when life was young, urges the narrator as the musical opens. He goes on to explain how two neighboring families have an unusual plan to make their children Matt and Luisa fall in love. One way is to build a wall between their two homes, believing that separation encourages young people to fall for one another.

Next they hire a bandit to attempt to rape Luisa, which they will stop in time, supposing that the trauma will further encourage Luisa and Matt to fall in love. The narrator plays the part of the bandit in the "Rape Ballet." When the boy and girl discover the tricks their parents have been engineering, they are upset and decide to go their separate ways.

Having been disillusioned by their parents, Luisa and Matt discover they are also disillusioned by the wider world. They return home to finally fall in love, knowing that only together can they face the illusions and disappointments of life.

"One of the happiest off-Broadway events in a season that has been happier off Broadway than on."

—Henry Hewes,
Saturday Review

Book by John Gordon
Lyrics and music by Clark Gesner
Starring Gary Burghoff

The daily trials of Charlie Brown as he tries to fly a kite, win a baseball game, or talk to the pretty redhead at school have become part of American pop mythology. Theatrical imagination turned Charlie and his familiar friends into a musical for an off-Broadway stage.

Musically, the *Peanuts* character first sang on a record album. Producer Arthur Whitelaw decided to take them one step farther and for $16,000 mounted *You're a Good Man, Charlie Brown* as a stage production. It opened off-Broadway at the Theatre 80 St. Marks in March, 1967. Within three years it had earned $400,000 with productions in Chicago, Los Angeles, Washington, D.C., San Francisco, Boston, and London, and with a national touring company. Was it the music or America's love for Charlie Brown and his pals that made it such a success? Probably both, since by keeping the book close to the *Peanuts* comic strip format, audiences could quickly recognize the stage episodes.

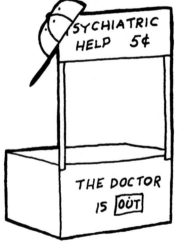

Book: There is no real story plot to the musical. Instead, the book is more a series of Peanuts-related problems. *The show opens with Charlie Brown's friends singing the title song. His lunchtime peanut butter sandwich and his pining for the little red-headed girl follow. Then Lucy bothers Schroeder as he plays his toy piano. Linus*

muses upon "My Blanket and Me" and Lucy imagines she has become "Queen Lucy." For a five-cent fee Lucy the psychologist counsels Charlie Brown. Together the children analyze the story of Peter Rabbit in the song "Book Report." In his imagination Snoopy flies the skies as a World War I flying ace on the trail of "The Red Baron." Charlie's baseball team gets "Up" for a game with their pep song "T.E.A.M." Lucy runs a poll about her popularity only to find out everyone considers her a super-crab. Snoopy sings "Suppertime," then, his appetite satisfied, howls with joy. Finding a pencil dropped by the red-haired girl, Charlie Brown sings of his "Happiness." The rest of his friends sing of what happiness is for each of them, then leave him, one by one, until only Lucy is left to say, "You're a Good Man, Charlie Brown."

Other sequences in the musical appear like the panels of a comic strip series. All of the stage pictures are familiar to fans of the *Peanuts* comic strip. The show's success could be considered a tribute to the popularity of Charles Schulz's comic strip as much as to the music itself.

"My Blanket And Me"
"T.E.A.M."
"Happiness"

Book by Dale Wasserman
Lyrics by Joe Darion
Music by Mitch Leigh

A major classic of world literature is *Don Quixote* (kee-ʻhōt-ee), written by the Spaniard Miguel de Cervantes (ser-ʻvan-tez) and first published in 1605. Cervantes's story deals with an eccentric man of La Mancha named Don Quixote who wishes to revive the days of medieval knighthood. Insisting on living by the ethics and seeking the adventures of an age that has passed, the eccentric don succeeds in finding only misadventures and ridicule. One of his best-known exploits comes when he mistakes a windmill for a ferocious giant, seeing its turning blades as the monster's flailing arms. The demented knight charges the imagined giant and crashes into the side of the windmill, much to the dismay of his faithful servant Sancho Panza. Such an irrational way of charging into impossible situations is now called *quixotic* (kwik-ʻsot-ik), the term derived from the name of our deranged Spanish knight of La Mancha.

The musical's charge at Broadway might have seemed as quixotic as challenging windmills. The inspiration of turning Cervantes's story into a musical began when television's Du Pont Show of the Month presented *I, Don Quixote* as a TV play on November 9, 1959. That inspired Dale Wasserman to adapt it as a musical. He asked Mitch Leigh, composer for radio and television commercials, to write the music to his book outline. Leigh worked for two years on the score, basing much of it on Spanish flamenco music.

After a pre-New York tryout in a Connecticut summer theater, *Man of La Mancha* opened on November 22, 1965, at the Washington Square Theater on Fourth Street in Greenwich Village. Its advance ticket sale was disturbingly small. Nor had any recording company offered to record its music. Nevertheless, in the spirit of a Broadway plot, the opening night audience rose and delivered an ovation seldom heard in a theater. Word-of-mouth spread and *Man of La Mancha* became the theatrical season's biggest hit. So successful was it that in 1968 it moved to Broadway and the Martin Beck Theater. Off- and on-Broadway performances totaled 2,328, after which touring companies kept Don Quixote in the saddle.

Man of La Mancha pulled no punches. Tough talk and harsh lyrics drove home its message. A single set without elaborate props, plus a story riding hard toward its emotional conclusion without the interruption of an intermission, underlined the fact that it was a show with a purpose, not just entertainment. This sparse staging has also made it practical to present it in summer stock and amateur productions.

"*Man of La Mancha* is an enthralling, exquisite musical play. The finest and most original work in the music theater since *Fiddler on the Roof*."

—John Chapman,
New York Daily News

"Man of La Mancha"

"To Each His Dulcinea"

"Little Bird, Little Bird"

"The Impossible Dream"

Book: *the musical opens with Cervantes, imprisoned by the Spanish Inquisition for writing against church doctrine, about to read his story,* Don Quixote, *to his fellow prisoners. To enliven his reading, Cervantes and his servant dress up as Don Quixote and Sancho Panza and the story commences with the famous windmill scene.*

Defeated by the windmill, the don claims it was a giant turned into a windmill by the dark enchanter. To challenge his sworn enemy the enchanter, Quixote must be dubbed a knight by the lord of a castle. So foggy is Quixote's mind that he envisions a run-down inn as a castle and the innkeeper as a proper lord. Quixote renames the inn's serving maid, Aldonza, his fair "Dulcinea."

Despite Aldonza's protests that she is a poor girl of sordid reputation, he continues to think of her as his lady fair. He confesses to his Dulcinea that his quest is to dream "The Impossible Dream." When mule drivers abduct his Dulcinea, Don Quixote rides to the rescue, finding her in a gypsy camp. Trumpets blare. His enemy the dark enchanter approaches him as the Knight of the Mirrors. The person is in reality a doctor hired to restore Quixote's sanity.

When the don sees his own reflection in his enemy's armor, he recognizes himself for what he is, an old, deluded madman. This return to reality breaks his spirit, and a dying Don Quixote rides woefully home. There Sancho attempts to cheer him up. Aldonza urges him to again become the knight, saying she is now his Dulciena. Aroused, the don lifts himself up to sing once more "The Impossible Dream," then falls back dead. The story is over. We are again in prison. Guards enter the cell. Cervantes arises to be led away to face his trial by the Inquisition.

Off-Broadway theaters became places for writers and composers to practice a freer creativity than that encouraged by the larger Broadway theaters. The three examples given demonstrate that off-Broadway musicals could not only succeed but last over long periods without the elaborate productions given midtown musicals. *The Fantasticks* continues playing. And *Man of La Mancha* moved to a Broadway theater to become one of the major works of American musical theater. Experimentation, enthusiasm, and youthful talent have made off-Broadway a major site for launching musical productions.

Screenplay by Bill Walsh and Don Da Gradi
Score by Richard and Robert Sherman
Starring Julie Andrews and Dick Van Dyke

Many feature films produced by the Walt Disney studio are musicals. The best have had their fair share of popular songs, including "Heigh Ho" and "Whistle While You Work" from *Snow White* and "When You Wish Upon a Star" from *Pinocchio*. Many consider *Mary Poppins*, a 1964 Disney release, the best movie musical of the 1960's.

The screenplay was based on P. L. Travers' stories of an English nanny caring for children in London at the beginning of the century. Most of the film involves live performers, but cartoon animation occurs when picture animals come alive for the singing, dancing "Jolly Holiday," and when a scatterbrained cartoon band joins Mary Poppins's tongue-twisting song, "Supercalifragilisticexpialidocious."

Two performers anchor the musical. Dick Van Dyke as Bert is a one-man band, composes poems, is a sidewalk artist, and joins the adventures Mary cooks up for the children she is tending. Van Dyke's angular dancing style leads live performers and cartoon animals in exhilarating dance sequences.

Julie Andrews had been passed over for the role of Eliza Doolittle in the movie version of *My Fair Lady*, although she had originated the part in the Broadway production. She proved her stature as a singer and actress by playing Mary Poppins, her first movie role, and went on from there to become a popular film star.

Screenplay: *The Banks family hires Mary Poppins, a kind but firm nanny, to mind their children. Besides being a competent nanny, Mary Poppins can also work magic, flying through the*

| "Jolly Holiday" |
| "Step in Time" |
| "Chim Chim Cheree" |

London sky with only the aid of an umbrella. Bert, an all-around handyman, joins Mary and the Banks children for their animated adventures. They and London's chimney sweeps "Step in Time" across the city's roofs in one of the most delightful dance sequences ever filmed. They also visit Uncle Albert, who is unable to stay earthbound when he laughs, and floats up to the ceiling of his apartment with hearty chuckling. All goes well until a visit to Mr. Banks's place of work, a bank, turns into chaos. When Mr. Banks manages to keep his job despite the disruption, Mary's work as nanny ends and she floats off to seek another family with troublesome children to mind.

Questions and Activities

Examining musicals

1. Why was it necessary for unknown composers, writers, and performers to begin seeking off-Broadway theaters in the 1950's and 1960's?

2. In your opinion, how important to the success of a musical is elaborate production?

3. What is your favorite comic strip? Outline typical situations from that strip that could be pieced together as a musical in the spirit of *You're a Good Man, Charlie Brown.*

4. Why is it easier for student theater groups to stage off-Broadway shows than Broadway musicals?

Listening to music

1. "Try to Remember" not only succeeded as a popular song, but helped make *The Fantasticks* a success. Why? Simply because it is a lovely song. Listen to it. Think about what makes it so appealing.

2. When the songs "Man of La Mancha" and "The Impossible Dream" are first sung in *Man of La Mancha*, they sound proud and hopeful. That changes when they are sung in reprise when Don Quixote lies dying. Listen to hear how the way they are sung reflects the changing situation of the story.

3. "Supercalifragilisticexpialidocious" is a hard word to read. Is it more easily sung, as in *Mary Poppins*?

Creating a musical

Act II, Scene *i*:

No longer able to perform, our star writes a musical, then after disappointments, finds someone willing to produce it in a small, off-Broadway theater.

1. Expand this story outline into a complete scene.
2. Pick songs from off-Broadway musicals that will be included in this, the star's first musical creation.
3. Choose simple costumes and props for this scene.

Reading the critics

John Chapman's review mentioned the "original" nature of *Man of La Mancha*. After reading the book description in this chapter, hearing the show's music, or seeing the show, what do you pick as its original features?

Sing

CHAPTER 15

The 1970's

Watergate, the end of the Vietnam War, the Camp David agreement between Egypt and Israel, and the Iran hostage situation. Did any of these major events reflect on Broadway? No. Instead, in the 1970's Broadway reflected upon itself, the Broadway of the past.

On January 19, 1971, *No No, Nanette* opened at the Forty-sixth Street Theater. Sound familiar? It should, because this musical was originally staged in the 1920's—as discussed in Chapter 9. In the quarter century since World War II, New York's theaters had presented some of the finest musicals ever created. Then suddenly the fountain of musical invention seemed to go dry, or, at least, run low. To save itself, Broadway dipped into the past, reviving old shows that had once won audience favor in the hope they could score again. *No, No, Nanette* did score big with the help of veteran performers Ruby Keeler and Jack Gilford. This 1971 version lasted for 861 performances. In 1925 it had stayed on Broadway for only 321 nights.

There were many more revivals. In 1972 *On the Town* was recalled from 1944. And in 1971 producers dug back only four years to resurrect *You're a Good Man, Charlie Brown*. It was true, there was no *My Fair Lady* or *Music Man* or *Fiddler* or *Man of La Mancha* to prance across Broadway stages. Yet the decade did have some good new shows that became important parts of musical history.

Lyrics by Tim Rice
Music by Andrew Lloyd Webber
Starring Ian Gillan, Murray Head, and Yvonne Elliman

Hair had demonstrated how rock music could anchor a Broadway show. *Jesus Christ Superstar* took new attitudes one step further. The closest that biblical events ever came to popular culture in the twentieth century had been in epic Hollywood films. But to turn the most sacred moments of the New Testament into a musical, then suggest that Jesus could be compared with a pop superstar, was a revolution. Many people thought it was an outrageous revolution.

Even the story of how this show reached Broadway suggests something of a revolution. Since the 1930's record companies had been releasing albums with original cast performances. These served as souvenirs for those who had seen the shows and introduced the music to people around the country who would never visit a New York theater. Now *Jesus Christ Superstar* turned the process around.

Two Englishmen, lyricists Tim Rice and twenty-one-year-old Andrew Lloyd Webber, had created a double record album with songs based on the events that led to the crucifixion of Jesus. Lloyd Webber's father was a teacher of classical music, so Andrew had been raised in a sophisticated musical atmosphere. As a young Englishman, he greatly admired the music of the Beatles, Rolling Stones, and other British pop groups. It was natural that he should combine the spirit of rock with traditional music in his own compositions.

The record album was very successful, with some of its songs making the charts. The idea of reworking it into a musical followed upon its success. Opening in the early fall of 1971, the musical introduced all the brilliant colors and amplified sound of pop music to a Broadway stage.

The show is described as a rock opera, but the music of *Jesus Christ Superstar* is not confined to pop styles. As do most successful composers of musical productions, Lloyd Webber recognized the importance of musical variety. He gave "Hosanna" all the power of a triumphal chorus in grand opera. "Herod's Song" is a musical blockbuster in the best Broadway tradition.

Many critics feel the Broadway version was not well staged. Production problems were solved for its much longer London run, which lasted ten years, the longest of any musical in that city's theatrical history. Like *Hair*, in every place *Jesus Christ Superstar* appeared, its staging differed. It was eventually seen in thirty-seven different countries, from A to Z, Australia to Zimbabwe, with countries such as Iceland and Yugoslavia in between.

Book: *The story of this musical retells the events of the last seven days of the earthly life of Jesus. Like a modern pop idol, Jesus has amassed a tremendous following. Judas, however, fears that worship of Jesus the person has replaced the importance of the message*

"It borders on blasphemy and sacrilege. I do not endorse the production. Nor do I urge young people to see it."

—The Reverend Billy Graham

"Hosanna"

"King Herod's Song"

"Superstar"

"Heaven on Their Minds"

108

he delivers. It is this doubt that leads Judas toward the betrayal. Jesus himself seems to accept this image twist, admitting that he is weary of his mission and resigned to martyrdom. The musical's song titles tell the rest of the story—"The Last Supper," "Gethsemane," "The Arrest," "Pilate and Christ," and on to the "Crucifixion."

Book by Roger O. Hirson
Lyrics and music by Stephen Schwartz
Starring Ben Vereen, John Rubenstein, and Jill Clayburgh

Charlemagne was the great French king who dominated Northern Europe in the years around A.D. 800. His son Pepin became the subject of the biggest Broadway hit of the 1972–73 season, when composer Stephen Schwartz and writer Roger O. Hirson used the period and its legends to create the musical. They played loosely with historical facts just as they played with the name, changing Pepin to Pippin. The musical's long run could be attributed in part to extensive television promotions, yet it had music and charm that justified its popularity.

> **Book:** *Like* Hair *and* You're a Good Man, Charlie Brown, *Pippin has little plot. It is a series of scenes without intermission showing Pippin's turmoil in his search for personal identity. The show opens with many hands, palms open, glowing on the darkened stage. Out of the darkness appears Ben Vereen suggesting there is "Magic to Do." He then uses stage magic to turn his performing clowns into the medieval characters surrounding Pippin.*
>
> *Each of the scenes charts Pippin's search for the meaning of his life. He yearns for glory in war, becomes involved with women, and champions social causes. In the end he seeks an ordinary, settled life with his wife, Catherine, content with "Simple Joys." Such a sequence could describe the route many people take through life, making it easy for audiences to identify with this man, although he represented a king who lived more than a thousand years earlier.*

"Magic to Do"
"Simple Joys"
"Corner of the Sky"

Book by Hugh Wheeler
Lyrics and music by Stephen Sondheim
Starring Glynis Johns, Len Cariou, and Hermione Gingold

In 1956, little-known Swedish director Ingmar Bergman showed his *Smiles of a Summer Night* at the famous Cannes Film Festival. With the showing he was no longer unknown. Bergman, who had written the screenplay and directed the movie, became one of the foremost filmmakers of the second half of the twentieth century.

In 1973 Bergman's film story came alive on Broadway as *A Little Night Music*, with songs by Stephen Sondheim. Sondheim's list of Broadway credits was already long, and included *West Side Story*, *Gypsy*, *A Funny Thing Happened on the Way to the Forum*, and *Follies*.

The title *A Little Night Music* set the tone for the musical as a translation of Mozart's serenade "Eine Kleine Nachtmusik." The story does not take place in Mozart's eighteenth-century Vienna. Instead, it is set beneath the Swedish summer "midnight sun" of 1901. Yet its genteel, old-world charm and light sophistication gives this romantic comedy that same quality loved in Mozart's music. Keeping with the spirit, composer Sondheim set much of the score to a waltz tempo. This led some critics to describe the musical as an operetta. However, its bittersweet cynicism gives *A Little Night Music* a depth not found in the usual sentimentalism of typical operettas.

Book: *The cynicism operates from the very beginning with the songs "Now," "Later," and "Soon," which express the differing attitudes toward love felt by the musical's principal characters. One of them, Frederick Egerman, has fallen in love with his former mistress, the actress Desirée. His feelings are complicated because he is already married to Anne, a young woman no older than his son. Count Carl-Magnus, Desirée's current lover, suspects Egerman, and so sends his own wife to reveal Egerman's indiscretion to Egerman's young wife Anne.*

All these love entanglements are overseen by Desirée's aged mother, an old woman who can tell many love stories of her own younger days. When she hosts all the couples involved at a dinner party, it is certain that the jealousies, suspicions, and concealed passions will spill into the open. At one point Egerman meets Desirée in her room, an uncomfortable moment for both of them. Desirée covers her feelings by singing "Send in the Clowns," the musical's most popular song.

In the end, Desirée's old mother manages to disentangle the entanglements to everyone's satisfaction as Egerman's son elopes with his father's wife, Count Carl-Magnus returns to his countess, and Egerman is free to be with Desirée. Having succeeded with her last manipulations in the affairs of love, Desirée's invalid mother quietly dies unnoticed in her chair.

"Send in the Clowns"
"Every Day a Little Death"

Book by James Kirkwood
Lyrics by Edward Kleban
Music by Marvin Hamlisch
Starring Robert LuPone and Donna McKechnie

Throughout the 1950's and '60's, records for long performance runs had been steadily broken. It was a musical of the 1970's that would top them all. The run began on July 25, 1975,

110

when *A Chorus Line* opened at the Shubert Theater. On September 29, 1983, it broke the Broadway record for most performances at 3,389. In celebration at that night's performance, it strung out 332 dancers in its chorus line. And still it ran on, not closing until it had completed 6,137 performances fifteen years after it had opened.

As had many musicals of the past, *A Chorus Line* took its theme from the theater world itself. Stage life deals with fantasy, but before the show begins or after it is over, its performers must deal with everyday realities, often harsh ones. It is this double life between fantasy and reality that creates the dream of theater stories. The book of *A Chorus Line* dealt directly with this theatrical mix, looking at young hopefuls trying out for the chorus of a musical.

The production was not expensive to stage. This operated against the Broadway tendency to produce more spectacular musicals. Without an intermission and scene changes, the stage featured only a mirrored wall at the rear, transforming the performing stage into the working stage of pre-show tryouts.

Book: *Seventeen hopefuls are trying out for the chorus of a musical. Zach, the show's choreographer, must select only eight from the seventeen. Complicating his choice is the fact that one of the auditioners is his former girlfriend, Cassie. Because of her lack of acting talent, Cassie is on the downhill side of her theatrical career. Now she hopes to salvage it by becoming a dancer.*

Zach's approach to choosing his eight involves not only watching the applicants perform, but also asking them to tell stories about their backgrounds and ambitions. Recollections of how childhood dance classes offered escapes from drab homes blend into the song "At the Ballet." The discoveries of adolescence become "Hello Twelve, Hello Thirteen, Hello Love." One dancer's memories of a difficult teacher inspire the song "Nothing," and another's concern for her voice quality becomes "Sing."

"Hello 12, Hello 13, Hello Love" "Sing" "One"

111

Such tales of youthful hopes and dashed dreams, frustration, optimism turned into pessimism, neurosis, and all of the problems that plague the insecure world of the theater become the story of A Chorus Line. The musical closes as the selected dancers join the chorus line to perform the show's final number, entitled "One."

Screenplay by Norman Wexler
Music by the Bee Gees (the Brothers Gibb), Kool and the Gang, Beethoven, Mussorgsky, and others
Starring John Travolta and Karen Gorney

By the 1970's the heyday of the original movie musical seemed to have passed. Only a film of Broadway's *Cabaret* had any success in neighborhood theaters. Released in 1972, it won Academy Awards for Liza Minnelli as best actress and Joel Grey as best supporting actor for recreating his stage role as master of ceremonies at the Kit Kat Klub.

If Hollywood no longer produced musicals in the grand tradition, it did make films that displayed contemporary dance and song styles. Two of them, *Saturday Night Fever* and *Grease*, made a star of John Travolta.

Like movie musicals of the past, *Saturday Night Fever* hung songs on a slim plot. Because it was the 1970's, the songs were in a rock style with discotheque dance rhythms the prevailing sound. Among the disco songs was "A Fifth of Beethoven," adapted from that composer's "Fifth Symphony," and "Night on Disco Mountain," based on "Night on Bald Mountain" by the Russian composer Modest Mussorgsky (mō-ˈdest mu̇-ˈsorg-skē). The disco dance rage of the 1970's made the movie a success, as did John Travolta, whose cocky dancing style launched him into stardom.

"Night Fever"

"Disco Inferno"

Screenplay: *When Travolta, who plays a young New Yorker with a boring job, steps onto a dance floor each Saturday night, he becomes king, the best dancer present, for whom others back away to let him move. When he meets a thoughtful girl who is serious about her dancing, romance blossoms. The couple run up against the frustrations of those who have fallen by the wayside in the big city. Their only emotional relief is at the neighborhood Saturday night disco.*

Despite the number of revivals and show failures—eleven of the latter in the 1978–79 season alone—Broadway still staged musicals of quality. *A Chorus Line* would achieve record longevity. *A Little Night Music* was a jewel in the musical crown of its composer Stephen Sondheim. And *Jesus Christ Superstar* introduced new composer Andrew Lloyd Webber, who would dominate the coming decade.

112

Questions and Activities

Examining musicals

1. The revival of musicals from earlier years makes many think Broadway has lost its creative spirit.

   a. What is your opinion?

   b. What other causes may have contributed to the trend?

2. *Jesus Christ Superstar* caused much controversy when it appeared. When its creators, Tim Rice and Andrew Lloyd Webber, visited David Frost's TV discussion program, someone in the audience complained, "The concept is abhorrent. The album is blasphemy, a distortion."

   Tim Rice replied, "If Christ cannot be taken into the streets, into fields and houses, then he has no meaning at all."

   Lloyd Webber said, "I remember the dean of St. Paul's saying, 'Please try and take Jesus down off a stained-glass window.'"

   Discuss their replies and state your own opinion about using the story of Jesus for a musical's book.

Listening to music

1. Many people have condemned *Jesus Christ Superstar* without hearing its music. Listen to its recording, then examine again the comments of question 2 above.

2. Listen to some of the songs from this chapter. Compare them to songs by George Gershwin, Cole Porter, or Rodgers and Hammerstein. Do the songs differ in style? Do you think songs of 1970's musicals will last as long as those of earlier musicals?

3. Recordings of the songs from *Saturday Night Fever* continue to be marketed. If you hear them or see the movie, decide whether they could be pop hits if they were introduced today.

Creating a musical

Act II, Scene *ii:*

After an off-Broadway success, our star has become a writer-director of a Broadway musical.

1. What type of musical will our star write?

2. Select songs from this chapter to include in the star's musical.

Reading the critics

Comment on the Reverend Billy Graham's criticism of *Jesus Christ Superstar* as if you were writing a letter to a magazine editor. Agree or disagree with the Reverend Graham's opinion.

Memory

CHAPTER 16

The 1980's

Much of America's attention focused on foreign affairs as the decade began. The new president, Ronald Reagan, called Leonid Brezhnev's hard-line government in the Soviet Union "the evil empire." The decade ended with the Gorbachev reforms and with Western nations trying to shore up the former Soviet economy. Most dramatic was the fall of the iron curtain and the opening up of one Eastern European country after another, while in some areas cooperation began to replace superpower competition.

If musical productions did not directly reflect specific political events, they did demonstrate the new internationalism that broadened the horizons of American life. Simply put, the three strongest new shows of the 1980's were first produced abroad and were created by non-American writers and composers. They opened in New York only after they had enjoyed successful London runs.

Doing the Lambeth Walk

Another British import was a revival—that is, it had been revived in London but was brand new to New York. *Me and My Girl*, which first opened in London in 1937, told the story of a poor London working boy who becomes involved with the aristocracy. It ran for five years despite the fact that two of its theaters were bombed during the German air raids. Each time, the show simply got up and walked to a new theater. And the walk was "Doing the Lambeth Walk," which was named after a section of London and became a popular dance in both Great Britain and the United States. Revived in 1985 in London, *Me and My Girl* had its first-ever staging in New York in August of 1986.

As for American musicals, there were few smash hits. Notable was 1984's *Sunday in the Park With George*, for which Stephen Sondheim's past successes drew crowds to the theater. He based this musical on the life of French artist Georges Seurat, particularly the two years when he painted *A Sunday Afternoon on the Island of La Grande Jatte*. The painting depicts people in Sunday dress enjoying an afternoon at a Parisian park near the end of the nineteenth century.

Pure American in spirit was Roger Miller's *Big River* of 1985. Based on Mark Twain's *The Adventures of Huckleberry Finn*, it came to New York by way of the American Repertory Theater at Harvard University.

The biggest American hit in 1985, however, was *The King and I* (from 1951) starring Broadway's original king, Yul Brynner. The musical only closed when Brynner became ill, then died. Revivals continued to serve Broadway. In 1988 *Anything Goes* from a half century earlier was brought back to life to play the entire season.

Throughout the decade, *A Chorus Line* continued its record run. What had happened to innovative Broadway? It seemed production costs had become so high that producers were not willing to gamble on shows that might fail. So they staged shows by an established name like Sondheim or drew upon successes of the past, such as *Anything Goes*.

Or they drew on a name that seemed to produce successes, and that name was Andrew Lloyd Webber, the young British composer who had created the music for *Jesus Christ Superstar*.

Lyrics based on poems by T. S. Eliot
Music by Andrew Lloyd Webber
Starring Betty Buckley, Timothy and Terrence V. Mann

American poet T. S. Eliot lived most of his creative life in England, where he wrote *The Waste Land* and *Four Quartets*, both modern masterpieces of poetry. A lover of cats, Eliot also wrote a series of poems entitled *Old Possum's Book of Practical Cats*. Eliot's book had delighted composer Lloyd Webber when he was young. His continued love of the book inspired him to use it as the basis for his musical *Cats*.

In simplest terms, Lloyd Webber set Eliot's poems to music. Favoring a rock opera style, the composer used rock rhythms and sounds for the musical's songs. Yet he did not stick only with modern pop; he also allowed English music hall tones to give *Cats* its voice.

"Jellicle Songs for Jellicle Cats"

"Jellicle Ball"

"Memory"

The show's cast had to dance and sing as cats might dance and sing, if they could. Their instructions from director Trevor Nunn were not to act like a cat, but to *be* a cat. That they were, slinking through the theater stroking unsuspecting members of

Memory

the audience, purring, prowling among the garbage cans of the stage set, then arching their backs as they began to sing. The choreographer, Gillian Lynne, who turned dancers into cats, has said it was much harder to design these dances and then perform them than those of *A Chorus Line*.

Cats opened in London on May 11, 1981. After a broad advertising campaign, it opened a year and a half later on October 7, 1982, in New York. The publicity may not have been necessary, for *Cats* proved to be a great hit, still running as this is being written almost a decade later. No wonder its advertisements claim that *Cats* is "now and forever."

Book: *As the show opens, cats crawl from garbage cans, old cars, and other back alley litter onto a moonlit stage, singing "Jellicle Songs for Jellicle Cats." Then each of the cats sings and dances its story as told in or adapted from one of Eliot's poems. There is Gus the theater cat recalling bygone glory at the Lyceum theater. Rum Tum Tugger becomes a rock star. There is Mr. Mistoffoles the magician, Macavity the mystery cat, and Skimbleshanks the railroad cat. But most of all there is Grizabella, bedraggled, down-and-out, recalling her glamorous younger days. Her story is a melancholy one of misery, loneliness, and unhappiness with the other cats long shunning her. Cat celebration erupts in the moonlight bash of the "Jellicle Ball." Yet it is Grizabella's sadness which closes it all as she sings "Memory," the one lyric not derived from an Eliot poem, but written by show director Trevor Nunn.*

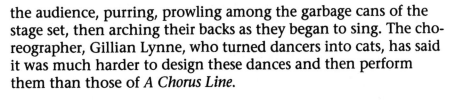

Book by Alain Boubil
English lyrics by Herbert Kretzmer
Music by Claude-Michel Schönberg
Starring Colin Wilkinson and Terrence Mann

Adapting a nineteenth-century literary classic for the musical stage was not a new idea. Two Charles Dickens novels had been made into the successful *Oliver!* and *Nicholas Nickleby*. The high adventure, vivid characterizations, and broad social panoramas of nineteenth-century literature provide ample material for musical adaptations. Few books are as broad and vivid and adventurous as Victor Hugo's 1,000-plus page novel *Les Misérables*.

As a musical, *Les Misérables* first came to life on records, as had *Jesus Christ Superstar* a decade earlier. Then Claude-Michel Schönberg and Alain Boubil staged it as a musical in a Paris sports arena in 1980. By 1985 it had been adapted and staged in London by Trevor Nunn of the Royal Shakespeare Company, who had also directed *Cats*. On March 12, 1987, it opened in New York with a ticket price of $50. Despite the high cost, *Les Misérables* sold $11 million worth of tickets for the Broadway show before it even opened!

117

Did the audience get its money's worth? Considering its continued run into the 1990's, during which more than two and a half million people had seen it on Broadway alone and another sixteen million worldwide in a total of twenty-three productions, it would seem so. Musical hours alone—three and a half hours of performing time—would suggest audiences got their listening value. With most of the text sung and the whole score woven with solos, duets, and chorus songs, *Les Misérables* is as much opera as musical. The themes, too, are operatic—revolution, justice and injustice, poverty, love, and death.

Book: *The book's plot makes a visual and musical journey through Hugo's novel, one of the great epics of French and world literature. At the opening, set in France in 1815, vagrant Jean Valjean is arrested by the police detective Javert for a minor crime. When finally released, Valjean's lot continues to be desperate; he is taken in by the Bishop of Digne. Tempted into another theft, Valjean is again arrested, but freed through the bishop's intervention. Javert, however, swears to hunt down Valjean.*

As years pass, Valjean earns respect and relative prosperity, although Javert still haunts him. It is 1832 and Valjean becomes involved in a student revolt. He joins the revolutionaries behind the barricades of tumbled barrels, wooden railings, discarded trunks, and broken timber. The revolt crushed, Valjean is pursued by the police once more, again with Javert leading them on. Valjean descends into the sewers of Paris—one of the most dramatic scenes in literature—attempting escape through the rat-infested waters pouring along the sewer tunnels. Finally face to face with Javert, Valjean knows the lifelong chase is over. But the detective, realizing that Jean Valjean is the better person, releases him to live out his life as a free man.

Book by Richard Stilgoe and Andrew Lloyd Webber
Lyrics by Charles Hart and Richard Stilgoe
Music by Andrew Lloyd Webber
Starring Michael Crawford, Sarah Brightman, and Steve Barton

In 1925 Lon Chaney, the legendary Hollywood actor of silent horror movies, filmed *The Phantom of the Opera*. In October of 1986 the story opened as a musical in London. Its arrival had been anticipated through television promotion that had begun as early as the previous Christmas season. By the time *The Phantom of the Opera* reached Broadway's Majestic Theater on January 26, 1988, $20 million worth of tickets had already been sold in advance of its opening—a record sale.

The musical had begun in Lloyd Webber's mind as another rock opera, the style of his earlier musicals. His first thought had been to treat the title song as a rock number and to cast a rock star as the Phantom. However, as his creation developed, the rock element lessened and the score grew more and more operatic. The title song took on the musical coloration of a full symphony orchestra with organ, all driven by a rock beat, which made a combination of great musical power.

One day as the composer was visiting the studio where his wife was singing, he heard another vocalist in a nearby studio. That singer was Michael Crawford, a performer in many musicals and plays, including the movie version of *Hello, Dolly!*, in which he played the young Cornelius. Crawford had started vocal lessons as he began singing more mature roles. From this chance meeting with Lloyd Webber he won the role of the Phantom.

Book: *In a brief prologue set at a 1905 auction of the properties of the Paris Opera House, Raoul, the Vicomte de Chagny, purchases a music box that sets him reminiscing about Christine, the woman he had loved. An orchestral transition flashes time back to 1881 at a rehearsal for the opera* Hannibal. *As leading soprano Carlotta sings, a backdrop crashes to the floor, frightening members of the ballet and chorus into thinking it is the work of the Phantom. Carlotta, refusing to perform, is replaced by Christine, a chorus girl. Raoul, one of the theater's new backers, recognizes Christine as a childhood friend.*

After her successful performance, Christine is drawn through her dressing-room mirror by the Phantom. The two descend into a labyrinth beneath the theater and cross a lake to the Phantom's lair. There he composes music for her, letting her know that it is he who has given her voice and inspired her as the angel of music. Christine tears the mask from the Phantom's face, revealing his hideous features, and thus tying herself to the curse of the Phantom.

Returned to the opera house, the Phantom lets it be known that he wants Christine to sing the lead in the opera Il Muto. *Nevertheless, the role is given to the more famous Carlotta. At the conclusion of* Il Muto, *the Phantom's curse sends the great chandelier of the opera house crashing to the stage at the feet of the performers.*

The Phantom next insists that the theater perform his opera Don Juan Triumphant, *with Christine singing the lead. At the premiere, the theater management and police set a trap to capture the Phantom. During the performance, Signor Piangi, playing Don Juan, is killed by the Phantom, who replaces him, though no one is aware of the change. When Christine realizes it is the Phantom singing, she snatches off his mask, revealing his deformed face. The police charge the stage. The Phantom whips his cloak over Christine and the two disappear. He flees with Christine to his lair across the underground lake with an angry mob in pursuit. Before they arrive, Raoul appears to rescue Christine. As the mob approaches, the Phantom releases Christine to Raoul, then disappears.*

119

This account of the plot of *The Phantom of the Opera* suggests that, along with the grand operatic score, special scenic effects played a part in the show's visual excitement. To achieve this the theater management excavated beneath the stage to house the equipment that raised and lowered the labyrinth and underground lake. The falling chandelier, a dramatic part of the original silent movie, was as spectacular in the live musical version, crashing toward the audience, only to be raised, and ready to crash again at the next performance.

Special stage effects can be spectacular, if they do not go wrong. Crawford recalls one night's performance. The boat in which he, as the Phantom, carried Christine across the underground lake was operated by radio control, much like an automatic toy car. One evening the boat suddenly stopped before reaching stage center. Realizing the problem, Crawford the Phantom lifted Christine from the boat as they continued singing, and began walking forward. Suddenly the boat began moving again, nearly knocking the couple over—which could have become slapstick comedy at a very dramatic moment.

Some critics have claimed that *The Phantom of the Opera* is neither a rock opera nor a musical. Instead, it is an opera, an apparently outdated form of musical theater. Yet, that seems appropriate, for its story takes place in a nineteenth-century opera house. Just as Rodgers and Hammerstein used a waltz to set the period atmosphere for *Carousel*, Lloyd Webber used operatic music to create the musical atmosphere of his work.

And is opera really outdated? Not if *The Phantom of the Opera* is an opera, for after five years it continues to play, already having drawn an audience in twelve productions worldwide of fourteen million people.

If history sees the decade of the 1980's as a turning point in international affairs with the political changes in Eastern Europe and Eurasia, the same might be said of the American musical. With the most successful traditional musicals consisting of revivals and the best original shows imported from abroad, it would seem to be a new sort of Broadway.

Does this trend for reviving old musicals and importing new ones continue in the 1990's? That must be left for you, the reader, to find out. But the next chapter can get you started as you watch for new Broadway shows and melodies in the present decade.

Questions and Activities

Examining musicals

1. The books for the decade's three major musicals drew on unusual sources. Think about them and about what similar sources you would use for a show.

    a. What book of poems do you like that could be adapted for a musical?

    b. What nineteenth-century novel would you choose as a basis for a musical?

    c. Can you think of any thriller movie that could be adapted as a musical? Briefly explain how you would do it.

2. Discuss ways in which the decade's successful musicals differed from traditional shows.

3. Why should European composers be having greater success than American creators of musicals?

Listening to music

This book discusses three Andrew Lloyd Webber works, two in this chapter and one in the previous chapter. Listen to them and to any other Lloyd Webber musicals, such as *Evita* or *Aspects of Love*. His song styles range from pop to opera. Only George Gershwin and Leonard Bernstein also composed over such a wide range of musical styles.

Creating a musical

Act II, Scene *iii*:

The star of our history musical has given up writing and directing shows. At last well off, our star now finances and produces musicals.

1. Which musicals, either new or revivals, will our star produce in the 1980's?

2. Select songs from 1980's musicals to be sung in the shows our star produces.

Reading the critics

Discuss *Newsweek*'s comments on *Cats*. Why are the qualities of "guts" and "flair" not usually found together?

???

CHAPTER 17

The 1990's

The 1990's, the century's last decade, began with a great deal of hope. The Cold War was over and Eastern Europe and the former Soviet Union began making the change to free market economies. It appeared as if the political worries of the past forty years had disappeared. However, as the old Soviet Union broke up into new, independent nations, armed conflicts broke out between ethnic minority groups. The same occurred in Yugoslavia, as that former communist state came apart, with the Serbian-dominated central government fighting each separation as it occurred.

In other countries, tensions arose from minority groups seeking greater political and economic control of their lives.

Book and lyrics by Alain Boubil
Music by Claude-Michel Schönberg
Starring Jonathan Pryce, Simon Bowman, and Lea Salonga

The first big musical of the decade caused ethnic tensions of its own. Claude-Michel Schönberg and Alain Boubil had followed up their successful *Les Misérables* with another London hit, *Miss Saigon*. The musical was a very close reworking of Puccini's well-known opera *Madame Butterfly*. Boubil brought the book up to date by setting the East-West love affair in the midst of the Vietnam War. That in itself was timely, as Americans still agonized over aspects of that war even though it had occurred a generation earlier. The public even worried that American servicemen might still be alive in Vietnam.

However, it was not the Vietnam setting of *Miss Saigon* that caused trouble. Instead, it was an ethnic question. In the smash London production, British actor Jonathan Pryce played the part of a Eurasian. When it was announced that *Miss Saigon* would open in New York in the spring of 1991 with Pryce continuing in his role, howls of protest arose. Asian-American actors complained that it was not proper for a white European in makeup to play the role. Actor's Equity, the American performers' union, threatened to deny Pryce the working papers he needed in order to perform in the New York production, even though some forty Asian actors would have parts in the show.

Despite advance ticket sales of $25 million, producer Cameron Mackintosh canceled the show. He felt Pryce should have the role based on talent, not race. In time, Actor's Equity gave in and *Miss Saigon* opened in New York.

> **Book:** *Kim is a Vietnamese bar girl working in a Saigon club during the Vietnam War. "The Engineer," a Eurasian resident of the war-torn city, introduces her to Chris, a member of the American military fighting the Vietcong, and the two fall in love. The day comes when Saigon falls and Chris is evacuated with all other American personnel, leaving Kim behind. Kim hears nothing from Chris, even though she soon gives birth to his child. Years pass and Kim continues to be in love with Chris. Then one day he returns to Saigon, but with a wife. Kim's hopes are dashed and their love story ends in tragedy.*

The success of *Miss Saigon* demonstrated that two trends of the 1980's had continued into the new decade. First, this was again a musical that had been written by Europeans and had its initial success in Europe before coming to Broadway. The other factor was the expense of supporting its spectacular production. It took $11 million to get it on the New York stage. However, that was quickly taken care of with a record $37 million advance ticket sale. Even after the show opened it required $500,000 a week for operating costs.

Miss Saigon was not the only London show to come to New York in the new decade. Andrew Lloyd Webber brought his *Aspects of Love* to Broadway in 1990. *Buddy*, a 1990 British import about the life of Buddy Holly, used the early American rock star's music for its score.

A popular 1920 Gershwin musical, *Oh, Kay!*, with book by Guy Bolton and P. G. Wodehouse, returned again to Broadway in 1990. So did *Fiddler on the Roof*. *Guys and Dolls* opened to sellout audiences in 1992.

After a record 6,137 Broadway performances, *A Chorus Line* closed on April 28, 1990, with many members of the original cast sitting in the audience. *Cats*, *Les Misérables*, and *The Phantom of the Opera* continued into the new decade. Meanwhile, down in

"The Last Night of the World"

"Please"

"If You Want to Die in the End"

Greenwich Village's Sullivan Street Playhouse, *The Fantasticks* was still playing after thirty years.

So began the 1990's, with shows from London and revivals of past American hits. This interest in revivals suggests that a great number of American musicals have become a permanent part of theatrical life. This is similar to what has happened to European opera and operetta. The twentieth century saw the American musical develop into a special kind of musical theater presentation with lively dancing, songs of many styles, comedy, and high spirits. The best of them can now be staged not only on Broadway but in theaters throughout the country and the world, just as operas and operettas are.

That does not mean that there will be no new shows. New operas and operettas continue to be written. The same is true of musicals—which leaves the rest of the decade up to you. What shows will become smash hits on Broadway as the 1990's continue? You will read about them in newspapers and magazines or hear about them on television's entertainment news. You may even be lucky enough to see a new musical hit.

Questions and Activities

Examining musicals

1. How was *Miss Saigon*'s appearance timely in the political history of the decade?

2. What is your opinion in the dispute over whether an Asian should have played the Eurasian role in *Miss Saigon*? How do you feel about casting a role with a performer of a different race than the part calls for? Use these two examples in your discussion.

    a. Could a white performer be cast as either Porgy or Bess in Gershwin's *Porgy and Bess*?

    b. Pearl Bailey and an all African-American cast successfully replaced an all-white cast in *Hello, Dolly!*

3. Does the continued trend of only foreign musicals and revivals succeeding on Broadway indicate anything about political or economic conditions of the 1990's?

4. Foreign countries such as England and France subsidize theaters and new productions. What is your opinion of federally-subsidized theater?

Listening to music

1. The story of *Miss Saigon* follows closely that of the Puccini opera *Madame Butterfly*. If you are able, listen to the music of both and discuss the differences.

2. Listen to the songs of Buddy Holly. His recordings are more than thirty years old. Could they be popular today?

3. Musicals are first of all about music. Are you able to find recordings of the songs and scores of any of this decade's new shows? Listen to them to decide what is happening in the musical theater today.

4. Instead of a title song, this chapter has three question marks (???). Select a song title from a musical of the 1990's to fit the chapter.

Creating a musical

Act II, Final Scene:

Some critics complain that the American musical is dead. Is that true? Does the star of your musical history die in the final scene? Or does some miracle revive your star so that your musical ends in triumph and the chorus sings a song of joy rather than despair? You decide how your musical ends.

Reading the critics

Collect some reviews of recent musicals. You can find them in newspapers or news magazines. Make photocopies, then discuss them in class. What was the critic looking for in the show? What did the critic like and what did the critic dislike?

Part III

The Show Goes On

The opening night is not the end of the story. For many musicals it is only the end of the beginning. With the increased interest in reviving decades-old musicals, many shows, gone but not forgotten, have come to life again. Even when not at home on Broadway, many musicals are alive on some stage elsewhere. To conclude our investigation into the wonderful world of musicals, let us see what happens after the curtain closes on opening night.

CHAPTER 18

Musicals After Broadway

The first time Broadway audiences heard this chapter's title song was on December 30, 1948, the night Cole Porter's *Kiss Me Kate* opened at the New Century Theater. The opening night of a new musical is an exciting time for the audience, cast, and creators of the show. But then what happens to the show?

The critics: The first thing occurs even before the curtain falls and the cast takes its bows. At the opening night performance, several prominently seated persons leave the theater before the music finishes. They are critics, hurrying to write their reviews of the show before their newspapers are printed for the early morning editions. At least, that has been the way critics have worked for many Broadway decades. Today they are more likely to review the dress rehearsal prior to opening night and then write, but not publish, their reviews before the show opens.

All connected with the show wait anxiously for the critics' reviews, often staying awake until the first morning newspapers appear. An interested public also waits, for a review can help people decide whether to see a new musical or not.

However, even the most respected critics can be wrong. You read how Brooks Atkinson, the *New York Times* critic, wrote negatively about *Pal Joey* when it opened in 1940, only to reverse his opinion when that musical was revived a dozen years later. The critic from *Variety*, the show business newspaper, changed his opinion from a pre-opening review of *Fiddler on the Roof* after seeing the Broadway opening.

The comments of Atkinson, Louis Kronenberger, Walter Kerr, Clive Barnes, and others were scattered throughout the second part of this book. Such opinions came from the theatrical reviews that are regular features of influential newspapers and magazines. Yet, the public has sometimes ignored their advice to support a show that received unfavorable reviews.

If the public sometimes differs with the critic's opinion, or that opinion is unfair to a worthwhile musical, what purpose do theatrical reviews serve? A review places a musical into public debate. It becomes a subject to read about, talk about, and maybe see.

The road show: Once a musical establishes itself, a second production can be opened elsewhere. That means a second opening, with performers' jitters and more reviews. The first move of a successful musical is usually from New York to London or vice versa. *Kiss Me Kate* opened in London after its initial acclaim in New York.

The original cast often moves to the other city and a second cast replaces them on the original stage. Rex Harrison and Julie Andrews, the originals of *My Fair Lady*, carried the show to London while a new cast took over in New York. In the previous chapter you read about how bringing the original London cast of *Miss Saigon* to New York caused problems.

Eventually a truly successful show may have many companies touring both the United States and abroad, all while it is still running on Broadway. Six months after it had opened on Broadway, a road company of *Kiss Me Kate* was traveling the United States. In 1992 *Les Misérables* was staged in 23 productions worldwide. During this phase of a musical's life, it is still under the control of the original producer.

Movie rights: Only after the musical has closed might the producer consider permitting a film version. Until then the producer doesn't want a movie of the musical competing with the stage show. For example, it was in 1953, five years after its Broadway opening, that the movie *Kiss Me Kate* was released by MGM.

Winner of 10 Oscars

Some great theater musicals have become great movie musicals. Movie versions of such musicals as *My Fair Lady*, *West Side Story*, and *Cabaret* have won their share of Academy Awards.

Now the movie producer must take on the problems of production. Maybe some songs will be added or others thrown out. The film must be cast. Most movie producers like to get a familiar name into the musical. So Audrey Hepburn replaced Julie Andrews in *My Fair Lady*, although Rex Harrison and Stanley Holloway, both movie veterans, played their original Broadway roles in the film.

130

Summer stock, revivals, and amateur shows: By the time a musical has had a successful New York run and road shows have taken it to other cities, it has become part of the standard repertoire. This means other theatrical companies may now stage the musical.

It is then that you might see a musical in summer stock. A number of communities around the country have summer-stock theaters. These are small theaters which operate only in the summertime, often in resort areas. Most of their performers are little-known, although a name star may be playing the lead role.

Of course, musicals can be performed in theaters other than in summer stock. And new productions can be staged in cities other than New York. This chapter's example, *Kiss Me Kate*, was revived in London in 1970. And as you have seen, many musicals have been revived on Broadway itself. George Gershwin never lived to see the many successful revivals of *Porgy and Bess*, on which rests much of his reputation.

Amateur groups also keep a musical alive. Sometimes the groups are amateur in name only, since the lead performers may well have a good deal of theatrical experience. Even if a single piano must substitute for an orchestra, the enthusiasm of an amateur performance can mean the musical lives for another night. *The Fantasticks*, *Pippin*, *Oliver!*, and *You're a Good Man, Charlie Brown* are particularly popular for amateur groups and high school musical productions.

Production rights: Regardless of who puts on the musical, permission to do so must be obtained. The right to sing, play, or copy any song or produce any musical is not allowed without permission until fifty years after the death of the creators.

Early in this book, Gilbert and Sullivan's *The Mikado* demonstrated some musical-making ideas. Arthur Sullivan died in 1900. His partner William S. Gilbert died in 1911. Not until 1961, fifty years after Gilbert's death, could any theatrical group stage a Gilbert and Sullivan opera without the permission of the company holding the rights to their works.

If your class is interested in producing a musical, you'll want to know how to get permission.

First you must find out who owns the rights. It is often not the original producer or writer and composer. The rights may be owned by a music publishing company or by a theatrical agency. The album cover or the record label of a musical will tell you who owns the rights to the music. If it doesn't, then write to the

recording company itself to get the information. Your public library can also help locate the owner of the performing rights.

To get production permission, a theater group must pay the amount of money asked by the holder of the rights. A large, professional company will have to pay a considerable amount. A school that only wants to hold a single performance will not have to pay nearly as much.

The holders of the rights may also lay down certain requirements. Perhaps the original dance steps must be used or the original costumes must be copied, and so on. Such restrictions help to maintain the quality of the original work.

It can be difficult to get the rights to perform a musical. But once rights are obtained, a company can begin casting parts, rehearsing, hiring musicians, building scenery, sewing costumes, practicing dancing, and then, as does *The Mikado*'s Wand'ring Minstrel...

...charm your will-ing ears with songs of lov-er's fears.

in another op'nin' another show.

Questions and Activities

Examining musicals

1. Many times we can only see the movie version of a musical. If you see a film version, compare it with the plot outline of the book as described in Part II. How does the movie version differ from the original book? Do you approve of the change?

2. Where is it possible for you to see a musical—in summer stock or a touring company? Are there any local theater groups that might put on a musical?

Listening to music

1. In addition to an original cast recording of a Broadway musical, a recording of the movie version is often made. If you can locate both versions of any musical, play them to compare.

2. This book has mentioned many cases where a Broadway musical song has been recorded by a pop singer. "Hello, Dolly!", "Try to Remember," "Anything Goes," or "Fascinating Rhythm" are just a few. Look for several different recordings of the same show song, then decide which interpretation best fits the spirit of the show.

Staging a musical

1. From the information written on record labels or covers, see who owns the rights to a musical.

2. As an exercise, write to the persons owning the rights to a musical and ask what is needed in order to be allowed to stage that particular show.

You are the critic

On the following page is a critic's worksheet for your use whenever you see a musical on stage or as a movie. Your teacher may provide you with a photocopy. Or you can write your responses on a separate sheet of paper. Either way, the page should help you understand and appreciate what you are seeing.

Musical Critique Form

Here's a form to help you review a musical, whether it be a stage production, a movie, a video, or an audio recording. Your teacher can provide you with copies of this form, or you can record the information on a separate piece of paper.

Title:

Book by _____

Lyrics by _____

Music by _____

The book:

Source of story plot: _____

Book plot or message: _____

_____

Comic points in the plot: _____

_____

Use back of this sheet for a brief plot description.

Score: List a song for these categories.

Opening number _____

Best solo _____

Best duet _____

Chorus number _____

Rhythm song _____

Patter song _____

Reprise _____

Finale _____

(continued)

Musical Critique Form *(continued)*

Songs: Pick three of the best songs and write their titles in the three blanks directly below:

Song title

_____		_____		_____	
1. Do lyrics fit the story?	❑ yes ❑ no		❑ yes ❑ no		❑ yes ❑ no
2. Describe the music style:	_____		_____		_____
3. Does the song					
a. amplify emotions?	❑ yes ❑ no		❑ yes ❑ no		❑ yes ❑ no
b. describe character?	❑ yes ❑ no		❑ yes ❑ no		❑ yes ❑ no
c. create atmosphere?	❑ yes ❑ no		❑ yes ❑ no		❑ yes ❑ no
d. entertain?	❑ yes ❑ no		❑ yes ❑ no		❑ yes ❑ no

Dance: Do the dances seem original and interesting to you?

_____

Further comments:

_____

_____

_____

How would you rate this musical and its music?

_____

Index of Musicals

Index of Composers and Writers

A

Arlen, Harold, 70

B

Berlin, Irving, 52, 65, 66, 73
Bernstein, Leonard, 73, 74, 85
Blake, Eubie, 57
Blitzstein, Mark, 69
Blossom, Henry, 20, 53
Bock, Jerry, 93
Bolton, Guy, 53, 58, 66, 124
Boubil, Alain, 117, 123
Brown, Nacio Herb, 63, 82
Burrows, Abe, 81

C

Caesar, Irving, 60
Cohan, George M., 51
Comden, Betty, 73, 82
Cook, Will Marion, 50
Crouse, Russel, 66

D

Da Gradi, Don, 103
Donnelly, Dorothy, 16, 59
Dunbar, Paul Laurence, 50

E

Ebb, Fred, 95

F

Freed, Arthur, 63, 82

G

Gaunt, Percy, 50
Gershwin, George, 52, 58, 67, 124
Gershwin, Ira, 58, 67, 124
Gesner, Clark, 100
Gilbert, William S., 3, 10, 17, 20, 22, 33, 41, 49, 131
Gleason, James, 63
Gordon, John, 100
Green, Adolph, 73, 82

H

Hamlisch, Marvin, 110
Hammerstein, Oscar II, 16, 20, 37, 60, 61, 74, 75
Harbach, Otto, 60
Harburg, E. Y., 70, 76
Harnick, Sheldon, 93
Hart, Charles, 118
Hart, Lorenz, 16, 37, 52, 71
Herbert, Victor, 20, 21, 52, 53
Herman, Jerry, 21, 91
Heyward, Du Bose, 67
Hirson, Roger O., 109
Houston, Norman, 63
Hoyt, Charles H., 50

J

Jones, Tom, 16, 99

K

Kander, John, 95
Kern, Jerome, 20, 52, 53, 60, 61
Kirkwood, James, 110
Kleban, Edward, 110

Index of Songs